Growing Older: If I Can't Complain Now, When?

Growing Older: If I Can't Complain Now, When?

George L. Beiswinger

a *Mr. Grumpy* book
by
Mirage Publications

Acknowledgments

To Ginny, my wife, goes my deep thanks and appreciation for her support and encouragement during the preparation of this volume. Special thanks also go to those who read the manuscript and offered helpful suggestions and guidance, including former University of Missouri professor Dr. Wallace Ramsey, former Temple University professor and chairman of its Journalism Department, Dr. Hiley Ward, and nationally-renowned writer and cartoonist Ted Key, creator of *Hazel.* Ted, a friend for many years, has long been both a mentor and role model.

To William Greenleaf, my editor; Quinn-Woodbine Incorporated, the printer; and Mirage Publications, the publisher; go my deep gratitude and appreciation for jobs well done.

Cover Design by Louis J. Forgione

Library of Congress Catalog Card Number: 97-92616

ISBN 0-9661123-0-x

Published and distributed in the United States by Mirage Publications, 25 Jazz Way, Mount Laurel, New Jersey 08054.

Additional copies may be ordered from the publisher at the above address for $6.95 each, plus $1.75 S&H.

To Ginny, my wife

Contents

Introduction

During our working years, we were too occupied with earning a living, raising our families, adding Scotts Turf Builder to our lawns and, of late, worrying about whether we had selected the right long-distance carrier, to pause for a few moments and contemplate and question life's more profound meanings and mysteries.

The years passed quickly. Their fabric, woven from the fragile threads of relationships, failures, successes, tribal ritual, and tradition, leave us with only fading garments of memory. But, hey, lighten up, we're still here; it's time to live every day to the fullest, time to seek, to probe, and to question.

It's time to laugh and, yes, time to complain when we perceive life's little injustices. Do we complain too much? I don't think so. Remember, we couldn't complain during our formative years without risking reproof from our elders, while in school without being labeled a troublemaker, and in the military without fear of reprimand.

Complaining about our jobs or employers subjected us to the most horrible fate known: being labeled a non-team player. Who's going to hurt us now? Nobody! When it's time to hang it up, it's time to let it all hang out! If we can't complain now, when?

1

Seeing More Clearly Through Trifocals
(a Potpourri of Ponderables)

Where were 4x4s, sports utility vehicles (SUVs), and other off-the-road vehicles back when we needed them? Our nation spent billions of dollars during the past half-century to create the finest interstate highway system in the world. In turn, these beautiful four-lane thoroughfares are fed, interlaced, and interwoven with comparably-finished access roads and freeways.

Why, then, do automotive manufacturers allot much of their production capacity, as well as advertising dollars, to vehicles capable of fording roaring streams, sliding through jungles in waist-deep mud, climbing up (and down) near vertical cliffs, and running across jagged, elephant-size boulders?

More puzzling is why people pay premium prices for these goliaths, then, like sea-bound lemmings, subject them to torturous terrain in an apparent effort to destroy them before the first payments are due.

Among those who practice such bizarre rituals, it seems you don't rate until you've rolled over your Land Rover at least once. Even staid old Lincoln and mod Mercedes-Benz now have SUVs. Hey, get a load of that M-Class Mercedes with the motorized winch and pick and shovel mounts. May as well jump those canyons in comfort and luxury!

I've heard, but been unable to verify, that Jeep Grand Cherokee, Ford Bronco, and Nissan Pathfinder dealers, following the lead of blue jean makers who introduced pre-stressed garments, plan to offer pre-dented 4x4s for their urban customers.

Options will include ten gallons of imported jungle mud, sloshed randomly over the vehicle, and an array of dead branches, weeds, rocks, and plastic road kill, wedged underneath bumpers and door handles. Is that class or what? Buyers of more plain or standard 4x4s will receive local mud and plastic vines from Wal-Mart.

In Japan--and this is the truth--they have an artificial jungle and mountainous terrain park where participants pay good yen for the privilege of tearing out transmissions and catalytic converters on their new Toyota 4Runners and comparable vehicles of other makers--a kind of demolition Disneyland, you might say. Or, as my grandmother would have said, "Now ain't that something."

The Right Stuff

Americans can't seem to get enough of presidential politics. Is it civic mindedness? Or merely an insatiable interest in who's caught who doing what to whom, when, and for how much? On-going investigations of private lives and financial dealings of sitting presidents, presidential candidates, and top aspirants, is a national industry. It seems it's not who's most qualified to become our nation's leader, but rather, who's least culpable.

Republicans are already tossing around the names of Steve Forbes, Senator John McCain, and even Dan Quayle, as possibilities for the next round. Democrats are touting Vice President Al Gore as the one to lead us into the next millennium. If truth were known, both sides probably have their sleuths out there right now, trying to determine if one or the other opposing candidates cheated on a high school algebra test, or played hookie once and spent the day at the pool hall. Are they also already lining up their independent counsels?

Presidential selection processes vary little from one quadrennium to the next. After months of paid political spots, which convey about as much usable information as re-runs of "The Dating Game," we end up with two major candidates, one of whom becomes president more or less by default.

We debate candidates' known credits, debits, experiences, and philosophies as best we can, all without having any kind of valid, objective scale against which to rate their true abilities. Before the next big event, we should bring this archaic process in line with methods utilized by academia. That is, mental ability should be the prime requisite.

The Solution: Require all aspirants to the Oval Office to take and obtain an adequate score on the Scholastic Assessment Test (SAT). Surely the person at our helm, the one whose finger is on the red button, the one who must pose in the Rose Garden countless times with important visitors such as Richard Simmons and Yasir Arafat--surely this person should possess as much intelligence as is required of a high school senior trying to get into junior college.

Qualifying on the SAT would also have the beneficial effect of narrowing the field--quickly. It might be possible to eliminate primaries--especially if tests are administered prior to the New Hampshire and Iowa charades.

Think of campaign cost savings; it would also save us from countless sightings of hopefuls trudging through snow-covered fields, trying to convince farmers they know all about hogs and soybean production.

Those with lower SAT scores would be certified for possible runs for congressperson, state representative, or sheriff. We need qualified people for these lower echelons of government, just as we need good plumbers, electricians, and drywall installers. Not everyone should go to Yale, or even Slippery Rock.

But what about experience? Try getting into Harvard Business School on just experience. It's important, sure. But, first, you must have it in the ol' noggin. Candidates' experience should not be totally political, which is often based on patronage or machine politics. Successful free-enterprise activities should receive high marks.

Far too much is made of where presidential candidates are born or their humble origins. We haven't outgrown the old log-cabin syndrome; Carter was the man from Plains; Clinton, the man from Hope. Recent candidate Bob Dole came from a modest upbringing in the Heartland. Ditto those other Bible-belt immortals: Truman, Eisenhower, and Johnson.

We cling to the notion that the Midwest and South are somehow closer to heaven than those "sin-ridden, lustful, greedy, and iniquitous" areas on the east and west coasts. Let's rule out geography.

Unfortunately, even after meeting mental and experience requirements, I'm sure we'll still have future candidates touted as: The Man or Woman from Friendship (WI); Fairplay (CO); Faith (SD); Noble (OK); Ragland (AL--how's that for humble); or, for a real clean slate, Hygiene (CO). Pity.

Suffer the Children

Why do adults talk baby talk to children until they are nearly three years old, then wonder why they develop learning and language difficulties in kindergarten?

Why do today's parents let their kids eat anything served up by fast-food and confection purveyors, while taking pains to feed their dogs and cats only veterinarian-prescribed science diets, geared to the animal's age and nutritional needs? "Don't give Jujubes to the dog, honey. They're bad for his health."

Why do drug manufacturers, as well as makers of household hazardous cleaning materials, hire geniuses to come up with new ways to make child-proof bottle caps, while toy maker Fisher-Price, on the other hand, expends similar energies creating manual teaching devices designed to teach infants and toddlers all manner of manipulative skills?

A few words about modern toys: Voice chip toys and books are deterrents to the development of a child's natural curiosity. Why? Kids seldom get to play with them until the batteries are dead. For some strange reason, otherwise sane grown-ups like to push the picture of the pig and hear it go oink-oink.

After a "talking gift" has been unwrapped, pleas of the one- or two-year-old recipient for possession are ignored until the adults, under guise of "showing the child how," push the picture of the cow to make it mo-o-o, the duck to quack, and the hen to cluck-cluck. "How do they do that?" they exclaim to one another with unbridled glee, as they make the pig go oink once more. "Wouldn't we have loved toys like this when we were kids?"

Home State Disorder

What is it in the human psyche that permits people to live twenty years at the same location, without meeting neighbors on either side--or even caring to? But when meeting strangers from anywhere in their home state, when a thousand miles from home, they are greeted like long-lost siblings?

Suppose you, a Pennsylvanian, are visiting the Grand Canyon. As you back out of a parking space, you notice that the car pulling into the adjacent spot has a Pennsylvania plate. You stop and rush to the other vehicle, shouting, "Hey, fellow Keystoner, how ya doin'?"

The other driver, after making sure he's not being mugged, gets out, shakes hands, and asks where you live.

"I'm from Allentown," you reply proudly. "And you?"

"We're from Beaver Falls," replies your new friend.

"Beaver Falls," you echo. "Know it well. It's only about three hundred miles from Allentown. Well, well, it's a small world.

"Hey, what are you and your family doing tonight? Would you like to get together for dinner? How about golf tomorrow? Where did you go to school? Would you like to become executor of our estate?"

After exchanging mailing addresses, you pose for a group photo. And so it goes--this strange ritual. Then, shaking hands warmly, you go separate ways. But neither you nor the other party shows up at agreed spot for dinner that evening. Ditto golf the next morning. You'll never meet again.

Watch the Watch Hype

If correct time is all you want, quartz-regulated ten-dollar watches peddled from overcoat linings on 42nd Street, NYC, work about as well as those costing ten thousand at Cartier or Baileys Banks & Biddle. Why pay the megabucks? Well, okay, it's for solid gold, diamond-encrusted bezels, I can understand that.

But why pay heavily for such intangible and chattel-less amenities as certified water resistant to seventy feet, especially when you hate water and live in places like

Kansas or South Dakota, where the only seventy-foot water is in abandoned, rain-filled missile silos.

Of course, there are saltwater scuba divers who probe such depths and more, and they need to know the time, especially if they don't want to pay additional rental on their diving equipment. But they need to remember the watch guarantees say water resistant, not waterproof.

If these watches could talk, one might say, "I'm only at fifty-five feet, but, dammit to hell, I can't stand the pressure anymore. I'm through resisting." Gulp. Gurgle gurgle.

Never Water Your VCR

The Occupational Safety and Health Administration (OSHA) has performed wondrous deeds for our country. I have no quarrel with it. But hasn't it gone a little too far? Its rules, coupled with growing fears of litigation, have makers of anything, as well as consumers, scared to death.

I recently bought a screw driver. The attached tag said, "Before attempting to use this tool, shut off all power in house at circuit breaker, check for gas leaks, beware of slippery floors, and ask closest paramedic unit to stand by." Well, okay, not really.

But (and this is the truth) the litany of cautions that came with my new VCR said it wasn't good to leave it out in the rain or immerse it in water. I wish they had told me that when I bought my first one. I wondered why *Blockbuster Video* always complained that my returned rentals had to be drip-dried.

That's the System

It annoys me that everything is called a system now. I don't mean just things connected with computers. The other day I bought a shrink-wrapped paint roller, roller handle, pan and pan liner. Said an insert: "Congratulations. You have purchased one of the finest home decorating systems available today." They should congratulate themselves for having sold one of their systems.

Finally, since retiring, I wonder and worry about many other things. I'll write about them from time to time. Meanwhile, I hope you enjoy this original collection of essays. I believe they comprise one of today's finest reading systems.

2

Age Has Nothing to do with my Handyman Skills

As a retiree, I enjoy doing little projects around the house. I like to work with my hands. However, my loving spouse of forty-plus years thinks I take too much time on relatively small jobs. Nonsense. I'm as fast, agile, and dexterous as I've always been, and I can prove it anytime.

I was ready recently when she asked me to put up a paper towel holder in the laundry room. "It'll take me ten minutes at most," I said smugly. "I want you to clock me with this sports timer."

The holder was one of those simple plastic devices with folding ears at each end to hold a roll of towels. With holder and cordless drill in one hand, and the two short screws, plastic anchors, and a screw driver in the other, I said, "Start the clock."

I placed the holder in the designated spot, and marked screw holes for drilling. Then I noticed the screws had the standard slot, and my screw driver was of the Phillips variety. "Time out," I cried. "Stop the clock." **(elapsed time 1:20)**

After retrieving the right screw driver, things got underway again. Incidentally, the Phillips-head screw (and driver) was invented sometime during the late 1920s by one Henry Phillips. His motivation is unclear, but it was probably to delay wife-suggested household projects by claiming he didn't have the right screw driver.

Now a small problem had developed. The holder didn't fit flat against the wood-panelled wall. A small rise made it rock back and forth--wonder why I didn't notice that before?

Well, a few passes with a chisel will remedy the problem, and the shaved area will be behind the holder. "Hit the stop button again, honey," I said. **(elapsed time 3:07)** "Hanging the holder is only a ten minute job, sure, but I have no control over unanticipated obstacles. I'll be back when I find a chisel. Might have to borrow one from Harry next door."

"Okay, but you'll have to be your own timekeeper," she said. "I have a dental appointment and some shopping to do."

I didn't have a chisel, and neither did Harry. But I figured my wide screw driver would suffice. Being able to recognize the versatility of tools comes with age. For example, when you can't find your wire cutters, your wife's sewing scissors can handle anything up to gauge 12, but borrowing them for this purpose has its risks.

With clock running, a few glancing blows with the wide-screw driver was handling the chiselling chore nicely. Then an encounter with a hidden nail sent the screw driver ricocheting across the washing machine, cutting a rather noticeable two-inch scratch on the top. It rebounded into a small window, cracking one of the panes.

For the first time, I sensed I was up that proverbial paddle-less creek--in more ways than one. Stopping the clock, **(elapsed time 5:22)** I headed for the hardware store. Luckily, it had those little bottles of touch-up paint for enameled appliances--the right color, too.

The store also provided a new glass pane, necessary glazier's compound, and glazier's points (little steel wedges that secure glass against the muntins. Muntins are narrow--well, it really isn't necessary to know about muntins in order to live a full, rich life).

My wife wasn't back yet when I arrived home. After repairing washer and window (not timed), and bandaging the glass cut on my left index finger (also not timed), I started the towel-rack clock again. Honesty in marriage is important. I had no desire to renege or fudge on my ten minute promise.

My time-outs were justified. In football, it can take a half-hour or more to play out ten minutes. That I had taken nearly four hours was beside the point.

I now drilled two holes. One went through smoothly, but one hit something solid. As a professional, I was ready for this. I'll simply put the screw, sans the plastic anchor, into the "solid" hole, and push the plastic gizmo into the other. In my haste, I pushed it a little too hard, causing it to fall into the hollow wall.

The unneeded plastic anchor was brought into play, but now the hole was too big. That anchor dropped into parts unknown. The job could only be saved by a winged toggle bolt, and I didn't have one. I called time again **(elapsed time 7:14)**, and pondered my fate.

In past similar situations, I would have turned to my faithful bottle of contact cement. Perhaps that was the answer now. The cement would secure the holder; the two screws could be pushed through mounting holes for cosmetic purposes. Just then, neighbor Harry dropped by to see how I was doing.

"Toggles," Harry roared gleefully. "Got a zillion of 'em." Wow, I thought. This is surely my lucky day. With the job on the clock again, I placed the holder, and fully tightened both screw and bolt--just ten seconds before my wife walked in.

"Gee, it really looks great, honey," she exclaimed. "How long did it take?"

"Would you believe only nine and a half minutes!" I replied proudly. (for the record book: **actual elapsed time 9:37**)

3

The Charge of the (Sun) Light Brigade

Thousands of new retirees, who spent their working years in the snowy environs of the cold north, are now, like birds of a feather, seeking comfort, warmth, and renewed spirits in the Sun Belt. They're also being joined by many boomers, who anticipate ending their working years in the near future. The Sun Belt covers parts of ten southern and southwestern states, but, during this final decade of the century, the heaviest traffic is on roads to Florida and Arizona.

After spending several simmers, er, summers in each state, to experience each at its calorific best, my wife and I chose Arizona. Both states have advantages. Both are beautiful. Both are warm--very warm.

But my wife is allergic to mosquitos, and I find coyotes more acceptable as neighbors than alligators.

Also, Arizona's 7,000 ft. peaks, compared with Florida's near sea-level terrain, seem a safer refuge in case global warming melts the polar ice caps. You grow more cautious with age.

Retiree home seekers in both states are hilariously happy. That's apparent from developer-placed billboards along the highways. Laughing couples, who appear little older than college seniors, are shown gleefully on their way to golf course, tennis court, or pool. They bicycle, hike, dance, and fly kites. Retirement is depicted as a never-ending frolic--a permanent vacation, where you never grow old.

In both Florida and Arizona, arriving seniors find developers, builders, and throngs of real estate agents eagerly standing by to welcome them into their particular

Elysian (subdivided) Fields. If you have ever wondered what happened to former door-to-door aluminum siding or vacuum cleaner salespersons, they're now selling real estate in Florida and Arizona.

"Right this way to our twenty-three new models, featuring lifestyle amenities tailored to the active golden years." Don't express doubts about affording such opulent digs, and all attendant trimmings (read options), on your fixed income. Even though they don't know you, salespersons quickly move to squash such considerations by reminding you "you deserve it" or "C'mon, you've paid your dues. Time to relax." Dolce vita is their motto. Onward to contract signing is their cry.

Model Home Views

Prospective buyers should note that model homes always have magnificent views of mountains, streams, or lakes; homes they'll buy will have magnificent views of the neighbors' houses. Model home landscaping (an option), if duplicated elsewhere, would cost about as much as the home itself.

As prospects enter models, strains of Big Band music waft through each room from hidden speakers. Miller plays Moonlight Serenade and, once again, wives dream of evenings of elegant dining and dancing. Husbands dream of golf, and fantasize that such carefree living might help them regain their old vigor in the bedroom.

The deep-pile carpeting (an option) would easily swallow small animals. Optional ceramic tiled halls and baths, top-of-the-line appliances, furnishings, and decor worthy of being featured on "Lifestyles of the Rich and Famous," help inch buyers closer to positive final decisions.

Resistance fades quickly when the sales agent calls attention to the broad expanses of glass. Glass from wall to wall, glass from floor to ceiling. Glass in ceilings. Gushes the salesperson, "Notice that the builder has designed each room to take full advantage of ambient light."

"Sunshine and light. That's for us," I said. My wife, always the practical one, took a more considered view. "Where are the necessary drapes and blinds for these broad crystalline expanses," she wondered, "and what will it cost to obtain them?"

When model furnishing designers speak of "window treatments" they use the term loosely. Perhaps scant frilly valances or brief swatches of cloth, artfully draped over highly polished brass rods by someone named Fawn or Tiffany from a design studio.

Incidentally, Fawn or Tiffany are also responsible for things like the champaign bottle and two glasses teetering on the edge of the whirlpool tub (an option), real ostrich-feather canopy over master suite bed, and the strategically placed potting soil, seed packets, and spade on the floor of the hobby room.

The Sun Eliminators

Unless you are a palm tree or saguaro, you simply can't exist in the sun-drenched structures, as conveyed to you at closing. Not to worry. After becoming proud new homeowners, we were deluged by bevies of sun eliminator salespersons.

After signing the sales agreement, but prior to the beginning of construction, the builder urged us to add the low-emissivity window option. He explained that, against plain glass, the specially-treated panes would easily reduce our air conditioning needs up to forty percent. With additional costs at only around $3,000, and promise of a forty percent cooling savings, who could refuse?

After we moved in, first to ring our door bell was a drapery consultant, who figured she could drape our abode, including the highly recommended heavy reflective blackout linings, for about $8,000. She claimed such coverings would easily cut our air conditioning needs thirty percent. She added that inside decorator shutters would do the same, and cost was comparable.

We ended up with drapes on the back and sides of the house and shutters on the front. A thirty percent saving is certainly nothing to sneeze at. Next to call on us was the sun screen salesman. "I know you'll want to protect those beautiful and expensive drapes and shutters from sun fading," he said, indicating it was unpatriotic to do otherwise.

Sun screens are made from a specially-woven poly mesh which deflects the sun's rays outward. "I can do your whole house for $1,850," he said with growing enthusiasm, "and it's a safe bet it will bring down your air conditioning needs by twenty percent."

The awning and patio-cover man estimated his now installed wares would deliver another twenty percent drop in our cooling requirements; the landscaper said the heavy-foliaged bottle trees he planted in front of each window with an east or west exposure would add another ten percent saving.

Now we were becoming concerned. I'm not too good at dealing with percentages, but my Texas Instruments pocket calculator (sun-powered, of course) indicated our cooling needs had now been reduced 120 percent. Would we be too cool? Would we now need a little heat?

I'm happy to report our fears were groundless. Now, when outside temperatures hover around 110 degrees Fahrenheit, we sit comfortably ensconced, tall-cool-one in hand, in our semi-darkened quarters.

Artificial lighting is required most of the time, since our "window treatments" and trees prohibit us from benefitting from the builder's "design to take full advantage of ambient light." The air conditioner runs full time, but think how it would be if we hadn't opted for all those great added features.

On the hottest days, we take our cue from the little desert creatures that hide under rocks during the day, then come out to frolic at night. Do we miss the ice, sleet, snow, salty slush, slippery streets, heavy overcoats, and dreary gray skies? You bet your frost-bitten derrière we don't. And most of our fellow emigres feel the same way.

4

Movers and (furniture) Shakers

As a "corporate gypsy" for more than thirty years, I've had more than my share of unfortunate dealings with long-distance moving companies. I've heard of people who were pleased with their movers. They became lifelong friends and, for all I know, named their children after them and included them in their wills. But fate decreed none of that ilk would ever place its quilted pads over my humble possessions.

It has been my experience that consumers are generally exposed to movers on three levels. First are the beautiful slick magazine and brochure advertisements. Then comes the suave-talking move salesperson. Finally, at an appointed time, an activity gets underway which might be described as the move from hell.

But let's go back to the first level. In one advertisement, young, smiling, well-groomed packers and loaders assure a client that her K-Mart glassware will be handled as if it were the Hope Diamond. "Depend on our professionals," the advertisement proclaims.

In another company advertisement, movers who look like Harvard business school graduates--even though they are wearing coveralls and military-style caps--promise the customer her great grandmother's breakfront will ride as if on feather pillows.

Take a good look at the guys in this advertisement. You'll never see the likes of them in real life. Should you retain this company to move your own great granny's heirlooms, take a fond last look at them, too--before they go on the van. They may have survived cross-country, covered-wagon treks intact, but now they're about to encounter a real challenge for survival.

Getting the Agreement

The move salesperson, of course, is the first live person you deal with on a move. He or she estimates costs, obtains a signed agreement, and arranges for pre-move packing. Read your contract carefully before signing. See if the small print at the bottom says something like--"this is the worst pile of junk we have ever seen, and customer, by signing above, agrees to absolve us of all liability."

Most actual moving operations involve a big over-the-road rig and its driver. That's about it. The driver probably owns the rig, not the national moving company you read about in the advertisements. He works under contract to the latter, which also paints its logo in large bright colors on his cab and van.

Before the driver--we'll call him John--arrives at your house on moving day, he must first pick up his "crew." John might find one on a bench in front of a tavern, carefully nursing something in a brown paper bag, and another in a line at the soup kitchen. Other sources include the curb in front of city hall, and the state employment office. For your move, he selects two from this slate. We'll call them Roy and Scooter.

When the jolly trio reports to your abode, John immediately goes through the house and proclaims that his company's sales representative never told him there was so much to load on this job. "They're always underestimating weight to sell the move," John mumbles. "They do this to me all the time.

"I'm gonna lose money on this trip." continues John. Roy and Scooter, suddenly realizing real work is involved here, nod sympathetically. John now muses (out loud, of course) that it looks like his children will have to forgo summer camp again this year.

Feeling properly moved by his plight, you sympathize, then prepare coffee and Danish for everyone. You also supply their lunch, afternoon snacks, countless glasses of ice tea, dinner, a few beers, and their breakfast, after they have sacked out all night on moving pads in your living room. By now, of course, you're almost family. For example, wasn't it interesting to learn that Scooter was a rodeo performer before he injured his back?

When you express concern about an antique mirror Roy is carrying to the van, he assures you he knows his business. He then playfully tosses the mirror to Scooter, who, in turn, playfully drops it on the floor.

"See, it didn't break," laughs Roy. "But you should have seen your face. I thought you were going to have a heart attack." As moving company advertisements promise: "Real Professionals."

Incidentally, there was a time in everyday life when "professional" applied only to doctors, lawyers, and athletes. It had meaning and status. Today, that mantle is claimed by everyone from public relations practitioners to truck drivers who service portable potties at construction sites.

When John arrives at your destination, he finds two new helpers, equally as knowledgeable and skilled as Roy and Scooter. Should you notice any new cuts or scratches, John will tell you they were there before the move.

Pressed, he'll give you a claim form to send to the national company that insured the move. Its adjuster will call on you, inspect damage, and tell you it looks like it was there before the move. Your odyssey has ended.

5

Storage Space Vital for Oldsters

For whatever reason, say retirement or empty nest--you decide to abandon the old home place and contract for a new, smaller abode, you are faced with a number of construction options. Should you choose the more expensive tile, or the cheaper vinyl, for kitchen floor? Lighting fixtures, grades of carpeting, bath accessories, paints, and plantings, all involve decisions.

But take it from me, the most important option to consider is the one for garage storage cabinets. Order as many as possible. Put them along both sides, across the back, and hang a few from the ceiling--even if you'll have trouble getting the car in or getting out of the car after getting it in.

Why so important? You're no doubt already ahead of me, but here goes: mainly to store carpet scraps leftover from your new house, as well as those from all your previous houses. We now have pieces of carpeting in our garage cabinets from our last seven houses--anywhere from two feet wide to several yards. We could start a carpet museum.

Remember the olive-green shag popular during the late fifties? We have a large roll of that, plus several smaller pieces. If we move again, we'll have to add a small utility shed in the back yard just for leftover floor coverings.

Throw away thirty dollar a yard material? You can't do it. Do you know of anyone who does? Never mind that the garage cabinets cost more than the value of all scrap carpeting therein. Larger pieces are sure to come in handy someday as replacements for door mats or runners.

The smaller ones? Well, although it's never occurred in any of our eight houses, you never know when someone will spill something in the family room, and you'll need a scrap to piece in. And there are multiple other possible uses. That olive-green shag would make a great dog bed. My Weimaraner, Earl, doesn't agree, but that's only one dog's opinion.

Empty Baby Food Jars

While carpet scraps have top priority when it comes to garage storage, space must be reserved for other things sure to be of future use. Take the hundred or so empty baby food jars my wife saves for possible use as containers for small objects.

She says they're too cute to throw away and we'll never have any more. She's right there, of course. Our last baby--a boy--turned thirty-four last month; his wife is now saving jars which their brood has emptied.

I think my wife has too many, but if I say anything, she's apt to remind me again of three hammers, two shovels, a rake, and an ax, all sans handles, which have been our moving companions for the past three decades. But that's different. Good tools are expensive, and I'll get around to buying handles for them someday--perhaps soon.

Finally, consider my lifelong record collection of LPs, 45s, and perhaps a hundred prized 78s, whose space I must continually justify. I did dispose of my 8-tracks, but just because they don't make needles for my turntable anymore is no reason to throw away the player or recordings. There are places that copy old records to cassettes. I'll get around to having that done someday--perhaps soon.

6

When Parents Leave the Nest

You've heard of (and perhaps experienced firsthand) the trauma and emptiness felt by parents when the last child leaves the nest. You may have even empathized with those poor Clintons when their only little birdie flew off to a lonely perch in California.

Additionally, you have probably heard the term "role-reversal." That's psycho-speak for when, near the end, children assume full responsibility for totally incapacitated parents. But watch out for Mr. Inbetween. I'm talking about the period when still-active parents fly the coop, and the resultant trauma felt by left-behind grown children.

First, there's the kids' shock of having their roots abruptly yanked from soil that nurtured them for the better part of their tender lives--say the past twenty years. They no longer have a convenient and safe refuge when things go bad at college, or when a newly married offspring has an overnight marital spat. Their old rooms are gone, along with much of their identities.

But ah, the resiliency of youth. They adjust quickly. Then woe to their now distant progenitors. When my wife and I retired and moved to an active adult community in the southwest from our previous abode in the Philadelphia area, parting with two college-educated, married children was seemingly uneventful--well, for the first few weeks, anyway.

Then, slowly at first, but with increasing velocity, a new era began. The first sign was the arrival of UPS with a large parcel containing a game of Monopoly, chess set, cross-word puzzle book, and several best sellers. A large magnifying glass was included with the books.

"Did you get our 'care' package?" chirped our daughter during a call that evening, during which she spoke much louder than usual. "We know you have nothing to do now, and we want you to remain mentally alert. You know what they say about idle hands and using it or losing it. Also, just sitting there all day will make you depressed."

Pets and Longevity

We weren't prepared at all for what happened next, although we did have a short warning. The night before, our son called (also speaking louder than usual) to alert us that a dog was arriving on American Airlines the next day. "We read that elderly people with pets live longer," he said. "Wolf is a little older dog. We didn't want you to have to train a puppy in your condition, you know, retired and everything."

"My condition? You weren't concerned about my condition when you asked me to help you move just last month. Believe me, that piano wasn't light. And how about when you asked me to help unload the Ryder truck with the thirty bags of cement for your patio?"

Wolf (the mature dog) was everything we had imagined, plus 70 pounds more. Bounding playfully over tables, chairs, and lamps, he was certain to reduce our quarters to shambles in short order--probably leaving us homeless and on the street.

After I explained to the kids that this animal was surely the antithesis of kinds that extend life, and that mother wasn't especially jubilant over what happened to her grandmother's Waterford vase, they mercifully conceded our plight, and agreed to let us place Wolf on a nearby ranch--provided we immediately looked for a cat.

Recently, a retired Phoenix couple we know flew to New York, rented a car, then drove leisurely to Rhode Island to tour the famous Newport mansions. When their daughter in Seattle didn't hear from them for a week, she called the RI Highway Patrol to inquire about the possibility of an accident, and to ask about filing a missing persons report.

She must have forgotten that when she bicycled across Europe with friends several summers ago, she didn't call home for a month. Apparently, retirement of parents releases a long-dormant anxiety hormone in their adult offspring.

The young want to make sure their parents take their vitamins, get regular checkups, and not fall prey to the many scams that lurk everywhere to take advantage of retirees--like promises of a free aluminum siding job if the company uses your house for advertising.

They're especially concerned about our driving habits. They needn't worry. I have observed that the retired elderly are indeed safe drivers. They don't speed, and they perform a "vital" service to others by making sure they don't speed either. This is done by maintaining a constant thirty-five mph in all available lanes, at all times.

Concern for Health

Children want to know their parents are watching their fat and cholesterol levels. When I was young, cholesterol hadn't been invented yet. Fat was a much desired attribute--especially in children. Now, in a half-dozen decades, it has moved from virtue to villain. My parents and other relatives used to say, "If you get any thinner, you're going to blow away. You need to put a little fat on your bones (meaning a lot of fat). Now eat those fat-drenched noodles."

Another favorite bromide was, "You should eat things that stick to your ribs." I was well into adolescence before I learned ribs were not part of the digestive system. I figured that, soon after swallowing, food was divided into two categories. The bad, but good tasting, food like potato chips, licorice, and Jujubes, went directly to your elimination system. The good, but bad tasting, stuff was routed to the ribs, where it became a permanent part of your anatomy.

Back to the present: Is our children's new concern justified? Have we suddenly metamorphosed into a different state of matter? Any evening now, my wife and I expect to come home after a late movie and be greeted by a surprise visit from our daughter. I know what she'll say: "Where have you been at this hour? It's eleven o'clock! Don't you know there are evil people out there?"

I also know what my answer will be: "Aw gee, honey, the Smiths across the street are older than Mom and me, and their children permit them stay out until midnight--even on week-nights."

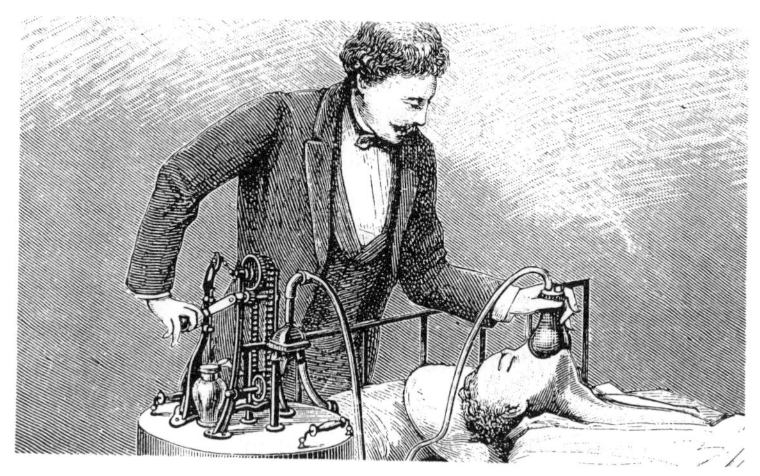

7

Modern Medicine: One Thing Never Changes

Retirees, more than others, have a difficult time dealing with health care. What with all parts and sub-parts of medicare, medican't, medigap, secondary carriers, and a plethora of managed-care plans, keeping your records straight is more foreboding than a prostate examination.

The practice of medicine is more complicated, too. Doctors, specialists for the most part, utilize the latest in electronic technology to diagnose and render treatments. Parts of their offices resemble NASA Control, with banks of monitors, scopes, and probes with flashing lights.

They also utilize trained assistants with unpronounceable titles like phlebotomist. But one aspect of their practice is as old as the Caduceus itself, and it appears there's little likelihood of change. I'm talking about when the nurse says, "Go to examining room three, take off all your clothes, put on the paper gown, and be seated. The doctor will be with you in a moment."

The waiting-time estimate is a little fiction nurses have perpetuated since Florence Nightingale first donned one of those funny white caps. Now, every time they say "the doctor will be with you in a moment," they wink at one another, knowing full well the patient will lose the rest of the day.

As a recent recipient of these timeless instructions, I meekly obeyed. The small, white, brightly lit windowless room is what I imagine a solitary confinement cell is like. I'm sure similar accommodations in our nation's penal system have inspired inmate uprisings.

After undressing and fumbling with paper gown to no avail (actually three gowns--I tore all three), I gave up, and mooned the lone, white-enameled metal chair. Brrr--it must have been borrowed from cryotherapy. But posterior numbness soon abated, replaced by growing anxiety.

Sitting in the buff in such surroundings for an extended period affects one's mind. It's important to keep occupied. The paper gown hassle occupied about ten minutes. What now? By keeping calm, I survived the next 45 minutes. I hope my experiences, and proffered suggestions, help others in similar circumstances.

Putting the automated electronic examining table through its paces, using its handy remote, can amuse one for at least fifteen minutes--even longer with a little imagination. Up, down, sideways, oblique angle, and a partial rollover. Hey, just like the tilt-a-whirl at the fair.

By raising rear half up and planting feet squarely in the stirrups, you can pretend you are an Olympic bobsled contender, or even a World War I flying ace in pursuit of the Red Baron.

After a safe landing, you notice the sphygmomanometer on the wall. Many an aspiring student was kicked out of medical school for failure to learn to spell this device. In this age of simplification, why don't they call it the blood pressure machine? No one knows. But one legend has it that a Dr. Sphygmo, its claimed inventor, threatened to destroy it unless he received credit in perpetuity.

Dr. Sphygmo is quoted as saying, "If Dr. Sigmoid can name his scope named after himself, while keeping a straight face, and without the slightest embarrassment, I should be able to name my more dignified meter after myself." Incidentally, Dr. Sigmoid is said to have studied under the renowned Vienna urologist, Dr. Seymour Upurs. But don't hold me to that. You know how these stories get started.

Unless you just like to see mercury go up and down, the sphygmomanometer has little amusement value without a stethoscope, and there isn't one in the room. That's because the doctor always keeps it draped around his neck, so other staff knows he's a doctor and won't ask him to clean the specimen room.

The little black flashlight with the funnel-like attachments is fun if you like to make shadow figures on the wall, but for utter fascination, scanning the big, colorful anatomy wall chart is hard to beat. I, for one, never knew my vastus lateralis was so close to my adductor magnus. I thought that was enlightening. And until I noted I had a teres minor and teres major, as well as an inferior vena cava and superior vena cava, I was unaware my innards had a ranking or social order. Just like the army or a big corporation, I guess. You can't get away from it.

There are many interesting things in the drawer of the white cabinet by the sink. Included are tape, gauze, tongue depressors, K-Y Jelly, and finger cots, which resemble little condoms--perhaps suitable as such for leprechauns. Your thoughts take strange turns after a while in these surroundings. Drawer material is sterile, so it's important not to touch. But I did treat myself to a tongue depressor, after noting on the wrapper it was peppermint flavored. It wasn't bad.

I spent the remaining time repeatedly taking my temperature with the digital thermometer, and tapping myself on the knees with the little rubber hammer I found on the cabinet. I got quite a kick out of that (a little medical humor, there). I have a friend who once, after an excruciatingly long wait, preserved his sanity by blowing up latex gloves from the white cabinet, to which he attached a length of gauze to make a punching bag.

Just as I was contemplating a similar activity, the doctor arrived, out of breath, clutching a bundle of files with multicolored tabs. It had been 58 minutes since I entered the cell, er, room. "Sorry I'm late," he said. "Had to drop my Mercedes off for warranty work, then got stuck in a traffic jam for ten minutes. I hate it when I have to wait like that, don't you?

"Well, how ya doing?" he called out cheerily, without pausing for breath. "How's that incision healing?"

"I don't have an incision," I replied. "I'm here for chronic abdominal pain. It's the same problem I've had for some time."

"Oh yes, of course," he replied. "Here's your folder underneath." He leafed through it quickly. "Hmmmm," he said to himself. "Hmmmm," he hmmmed again. When a doctor says hmmmm more than twice, it could be a signal for you to check your life insurance, review your living will, and look again at the pre-planning brochure from the funeral home. But a couple of hmmmms are usually nothing to worry about.

"Well, it looks like I'll need some additional X-rays and blood work before I examine you again," the doctor concluded. "Get dressed and see the receptionist to schedule these tests. Good to see you again. Gotta run."

After seeing receptionist, making necessary appointments, filling out medicare forms, and noting today's office visit is $60, I ran, too. Of course, I'm thankful I can get the needed tests, X-rays, and screenings. I've heard HMO doctors don't prescribe them. They just tell you to go home and rest.

Modern medicine. Every day brings amazing new discoveries and treatments, but the extended wait in the little white cubicle on a cold metal chair, sans clothing, appears destined for eternity.

Correcting the Record

Incidentally, after additional research, I discovered that the sphygmomanometer and the sigmoidoscope have nothing to do with doctors by those names, but rather are of Greek origins. I just wanted to set the record straight. No additional information was found on Dr. Seymour Upurs.

8

Dr. Koop, Please Don't Look at Me Like That

If I were extremely ill and had a choice of doctors, I would call for Dr. C. Everett Koop, M.D. I know he'd gladly come to my home at any hour and in any weather--black bag in hand--and, exuding confidence from every pore, expertly diagnose my malady, provide proper treatment for a quick recovery, then stick around for a little while to make sure I was going to be okay--physically, mentally, and spiritually.

His cherubic pink cheeks and white goatee, coupled with his all-wool-and-a-yard-wide, Pennsylvania-Dutch persona (actually, he's a native of Brooklyn), conveys the impression that surely behind his ample forehead must exist much of the knowledge, piety, empathy, and wisdom of the ages--the knowing and caring father of us all.

Yet, every time I look at his photograph (the one we always see in advertisements with the red bow tie and brown suit), or, perhaps more appropriately, when his photograph looks at me, I have this uneasy feeling I'm not living up to my full potential, I'm an underachiever--well, okay, I'm lazy. I want to say, "I'm sorry, Dr. Koop. I'll try to do better next time."

The former U.S. Surgeon General, and distinguished octogenarian, now works for *Time Life Medical*; you see his picture in its magazine advertisements for medical videos, as well as on point-of-purchase placards in drug stores all across the nation. I'm sure his appeals sell a lot of videos and help a lot of people. But back to my feelings of inadequacy Dr. Koop's mien always seems to engender.

It's a Look that must have caused me extreme pain and anxiety in the past, but when and where? After a long, painful self analysis, past parallels of the Koop Look began flooding my consciousness. The first encounter occurred more than sixty years ago, when I was in the first grade. I had forgotten my homework assignment and was told by my teacher to report to Miss Bertha, the principal.

To a six-year-old then, being referred to Miss Bertha was sheer terror. We had heard rumors she had an electric paddle. We didn't know exactly what that was or how it worked, but being cast into a lion's den would have been preferable to finding out. "I forgot my assignment, Miss Bertha," I choked, barely holding back tears.

Then it happened. Miss Bertha gave me the Koop Look; not an evil look, but one that said in this world we must all be responsible for our transgressions. No words--just the Look. After an eternity, she finally spoke. "I'm surprised at you. After all, you are an intelligent young man.

"Now I want you to write on the board ten times--I will never forget my assignment again." That was it--no electric paddle (although I scanned the room for its presence). But I am sure its pain couldn't have been any worse or more effective than Miss Bertha's countenance.

Reprinted courtesy of Bob Gorrell, Richmond News Leader.

I also remember receiving the Look in junior high school. This time it was my music teacher. "You couldn't possibly have practiced for six hours this week, as you claim, and still sound the way you do," he said. "Now here's what I want you to do. Practice in my office after school for the next two weeks. I'll sign you in and out." Again, the Koop Look and retribution.

I recall a severe example of the Look when I was in the army. This time it was my lieutenant whose gaze bore into my cerebellum for a good five minutes while I tried unsuccessfully to recite the first three articles of war. Of course there were other times in later years. They kind of blur together now.

Perhaps it was when I tried to explain to my boss why a report wasn't ready when promised, when I tried to justify a questionable deduction on my Form 1040, Schedule A, or when explaining to a traffic officer why it was vitally necessary for me to go 65 mph in a 30 mph zone. The Look was always the same.

The Koop Look! There's one for every age. It's the have you brushed your teeth Look, taken your vitamins and done your exercise Look, studied for your college finals Look, as well as the look your boss gives you when he asks if you would like to take another look at your expense account.

It's the do you have adequate insurance to protect your family Look, have you had your cholesterol checked lately Look, as well as have you updated your will Look, and have you considered a pre-arrangement plan Look.

I once interviewed former U.S. Surgeon General Luther Terry for a magazine article, shortly after he had announced the government's now landmark decision on smoking and health. I chided him about several well-broken-in imported briars in the pipe rack on his credenza. Smiling, he impishly replied that, yes, he too occasionally partook of the golden leaf.

Had C. Everett Koop been present that day, he would have given Dr. Terry the Look for a few seemingly searing seconds, then with fatherly indignation (kind, but no monkey business) said, "Luther, you know better." And after enduring the Look for a few more seconds, Dr. Terry would have picked up his pipes--rack and all--and quietly deposited them in the nearest trash receptacle.

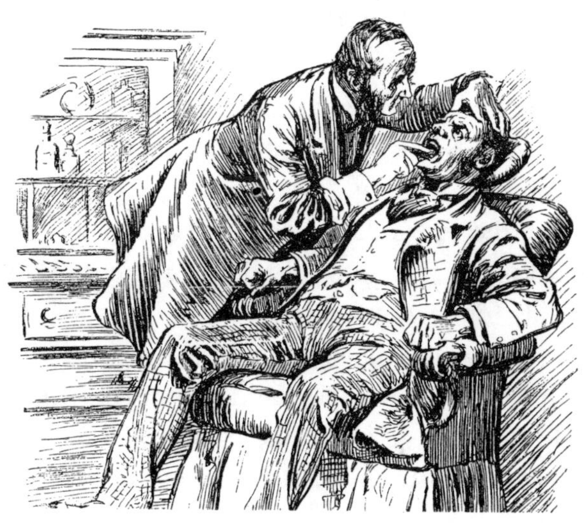

9

Dentists add Muscle to Their Research

Senior citizens need to keep abreast of what's going on in the world. They shouldn't just read AARP bulletins, Social Security pamphlets, and only those magazine articles dealing with liposuction, tummy tucks, and penile implants. They need to exercise the gray cells underneath their gray coverings.

I know that. That's why I paid particular attention to a recent news item in *The New York Times* concerning two dental researchers at the University of Maryland-Baltimore, who have discovered heretofore unknown muscles in the human head which extend from the eye sockets to lower jaw.

Given all the medical research that has taken place from the origin of Homo sapiens up to Chicago Hope, it seems incredible that everything inside us hasn't been found by now. But the medical profession has validated this exciting new finding.

Even the researchers kept their discovery secret for a year, thinking everyone would laugh at them. Well, give them credit for being perceptive. I'm sure such an announcement would have aroused suspicions that their patients weren't the only ones sniffing nitrous oxide.

Be that as it may, the scientific and business worlds must deal with this earth-shaking discovery which, in my opinion, rivals that of the perceived petrified worm on the Mars rock. It won't be easy. To begin, all anatomy books must be rewritten. NordicTrack, Vectra, Trimax, and Soloflex, until now secure in the knowledge they had all muscles covered, must now redesign their machines.

The new muscles were tentatively christened the sphenomandibularis. Because I can't pronounce that, I'll call them the sphenos. My theory is these muscles didn't exist in the cave man or in Adam and Eve (depending upon your religious persuasion)--not in their present form, anyway.

I believe the sphenos developed since the age of television. Semi-reclining on a sofa, and moving the eyes to follow Geraldo or Oprah, while vigorously munching Fritos, is bound to develop tissue between eye and jaw.

Evil Eye?

Of course the sphenos could have an earlier origin, which explains some of the metaphysical mysteries that plague us. For example, the "Evil Eye" has long been associated with things like witchcraft, voodoo, and Bob Dole (just kidding). Is this malady actually organic in nature, caused by contractions of the sphenos? If so, those afflicted need our help, understanding, and Prozac, not eye of newt or essence of toad.

Now that we know we have sphenos, we should learn to utilize them in some positive way. I'm not sure how. Properly exercised, the muscles might provide us with a new way to wiggle our ears. But other than getting us on David Letterman's stupid people tricks, that application is rather limited.

There's a possibility the sphenos might be helpful in a Jim Carrey impersonation contest. But uses will be found, followed by sphenos muscle strain, followed by sphenos strain emoluments, followed by sphenos strain emoluments endorsements by Joe Namath.

Finally, there are those who feel the medical community, specifically the AMA, has long known about the sphenos, but conspired to keep their existence from the public. Why? With more and more drugs available over the counter, doctors fear a sharp decline in office calls to get prescriptions.

They don't want someone to come up with a sphenos pain reliever, available at the 7-11. Look what over-the-counter Rogaine is doing to formerly $60 visits to dermatologists. If this conspiracy theory is true, it makes you wonder just how much more they're keeping from us. After all, they didn't tell us about the G-spot until the Age of Aquarius.

10

"Give Me That Old Time (but proper) Religion"

Often, when retirees move to a new community, they can't find a church of their denomination within commuting distance. That happened to me recently. That's why I decided to investigate picturesque "Old Ivy Church" near my home, although I think it was their published motto, "We've Always Done It That Way, but We're Not Fanatics" that first caught my eye.

Entering the church office at the rear of the sanctuary during one of my weekday morning walks, I was welcomed by a kindly white-haired gentlemen in a full-cut Brooks Brothers suit (or at least it looked like one). He introduced himself as a member of the board of trustees, and explained he had stopped by on church business.

"You certainly have a beautiful church," I said. "And such a lovely church yard."

"Thank you," he replied. "We're also a friendly church, contrary to vicious rumors going around that some of our people are a bit snooty."

"Oh, I'm sure that's not true," I said.

Real Burled-Walnut

"No, it certainly isn't," he replied, his voice rising, but still very much in control. "As one of our congregation put it the other day, rather amusingly, I thought, 'just because some of our members drive cars with real burled-walnut dashboards, and wear Rolex watches, water resistant to 70 feet, doesn't mean they think they're better than anyone else.'"

"Of course not," I replied.

"Try to be a little civilized today and you get nothing but criticism," he said, striking a file cabinet sharply with his folded *New York Times*. "Well, I suppose you would like to know something about our little flock here," he continued, pausing to adjust a pearl cufflink.

"We're really what you might call a fundamentalist sect, although not in the sense some faiths use the word. But everything connected with our activities, as you will learn, is directly linked to the Bible. I hope that doesn't bother you."

"Not at all," I replied. "Although there are a few stories in the Good Book that I find hard to view literally or understand. For example, when the serpent lied to Eve and God told it that it must eat dust the rest of its life, why were all subsequent reptiles made to suffer similar fates?

"Sure the serpent in the Garden of Eden was a low-down, lying snake in the grass, but because he lied, all snakes must now eat dust. I know congressmen who prevaricate quite regularly, and they continue to eat filet mignon. And, hey, why couldn't Noah have been more perceptive? How come he didn't notice both unicorns were males?

"Also, I think God dealt in a little overkill when he changed construction workers' voices to end the Babel project. A less drastic and more economical measure would have been to let them get the tower up to, say, three hundred feet, then start a rumor that the hod carriers had a better fringe benefit package than the stone cutters.

"The cutters would have immediately walked out. By the time things were settled, the building inspector would have declared the unfinished project unsafe and quickly ordered it dismantled. Of course, the multiple language thing has benefitted some enterprises. Berlitz comes to mind."

"Well, you certainly are a perceptive thinker," said my host. "The Bible does indeed present many mysteries, and believe me, even we here at Old Ivy don't have all the answers.

"But before you go, I would like to tell you about some of our activities which, as I said earlier, are all Bible-oriented. Believe me, we have a full agenda.

"Our Burning Bush Bowlers meet at a local lane on Monday evening. The Samson and Delilah Tennis Mixed Doubles occupy most of Tuesday afternoon, followed by the Mary Magdalene Ladies Duplicate Bridge Club on Tuesday evening in the parish hall.

"Our Gleaners of the Field Ladies Guild meets on Thursday evening. There isn't much to glean anymore. But they busy themselves by knitting warm mittens for children in Nigeria. Saturdays are a beehive of activity. The Jonah Men's Fishing Club usually gets an early start. Later, the Abraham and Isaac Father & Son Hiking Club takes off. Well, I've rambled on far too long and haven't covered near everything. Any questions?"

"You've been extremely helpful," I said. "You certainly are Bible-centered. But I was wondering--What about Sunday morning services?"

"Oh, yes, I almost forgot. We have a great fellowship. But you're always out in time to make your tee time at the club."

"That's considerate," I replied. "I would like to visit with you next Sunday and meet your minister."

"I'm afraid that isn't possible this coming week. You see, the Reverend Dr. Stringfellow Fisher Groton-White, IV, is attending a seminar in Cancun on new methods of touch therapy. Has something to do with the Laying on of Hands, I think.

"But come anyway. You'll be in for a real treat. Our Scriptural Interpretive Dancers are going to present their version of the Beatitudes. Actually, it will be their second performance while filling in for our pastor.

"Last Sunday, they danced their interpretation of the Queen of Sheba's visit to King Solomon. The queen was portrayed by one of our new members, a recent Vassar graduate. Majored in the dance, I think.

"Unfortunately, just as the King was about to give unto the queen 'all her desire, whatsoever she asked,' her foot became entangled in his raiment, causing both to crash to the floor in a rather unholy alliance. Two choir boys, straining for a better view, tumbled into the transept, sustaining minor injuries."

"Well, these things happen," I said. "I'm deeply grateful for the time you've given me, but I think I should visit a couple of other congregations before making a permanent affiliation, even though I do have a Rolex water-resistant to 70 feet."

11

Sex and the Senior Citizen (Being a farce in one act)

Senior centers offer many informational and educational opportunities. These include seminars and workshops on everything from health care, wills, and finances, to jewelry making, quilting, and how to lay tile.

I recently saw a posted notice for a forthcoming Senior Sex Seminar (SSS). Under the acronym, some wag had written, "Shouldn't this be (SOS)?" Regardless, my wife and I decided to attend.

Unfortunately, we got there late; it was almost over. So I can only pick it up from where we came in.

Program Moderator: "Thank you for attending our seminar on sexual problems and adjustments of the elderly. We hope you had an interesting and informative evening.

I would also like to thank our guest speaker, Dr. Dieter von Strudel.

"For those who arrived late, Dr. Strudel is a research fellow at the nearby Institute for Geriatric Studies, where his course, "Libido of Seniors Theories" (LOST), is quite popular.

"In our remaining time, Dr. Strudel has graciously consented to entertain questions from the audience, as long as they're not too entertaining, heh, heh. Any questions? Who has a question? Ah, c'mon. Okay, the lady in the third row has her hand up. What is your question for Dr. Strudel?"

"I would like to know if, well, you know, doing it, is dangerous after a heart bypass operation?"

Doctor Strudel, with wry grin: "I'm not sure what you mean? Doing what?" (scattered laughter)

"Well, you know. Just doing it."

"Madam, we're not silly teenagers who must resort to euphemisms and giggles. Surely your husband doesn't refer to sex as 'it'."

Puddin' Cake

"Oh my, no. He calls it puddin' cake. We used to play a little game. After dinner in the evening, I'd say, 'Would you care for some desert?' and he would reply, 'Yes, I'd like some puddin' cake.' But he hasn't said it much lately."

Voice from the rear: "With my husband, it would be shortcake."

Another voice: "Yeah, or instant puddin'."

(The room erupts in assorted yuk-yuks and guffaws)

Moderator: "Order! Order! Let the doctor answer the question."

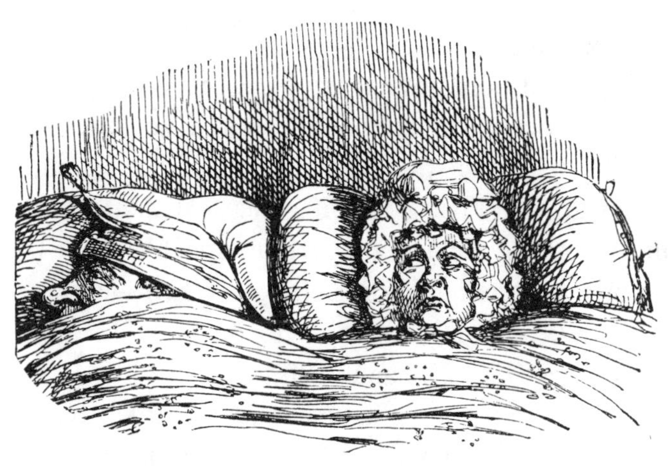

Dr. Strudel: "Well, we have done little research at the Institute specifically on puddin' cake (laughter again). When did you have the heart bypass procedure?"

"Oh, it isn't me. It's my husband Harold here. Wake up, Harold. The doctor wants to tell you something."

Harold: "Is it time to go home?"

Wife: "No, no, now listen to Dr. Strudel."

Dr. Strudel: "Harold, if you stick to home baking, you should have no trouble. But watch out for commercial bakery products. They could spell real trouble for your heart. Next question? Yes, the lady in the corner."

"Dr. Strudel, lately, the only way my husband can get turned on is for me to go in the bedroom and undress, while he goes outside and peeks through the window. What can I do?"

"Well, ma'am, your husband is obviously a very sick man. I suggest he find a good therapist. Also, he should learn to peek through the keyhole of an interior door like normal people. Who's next? Yes, the lady with the sequined tiara. What is your question?"

"Doctor, I'm at my wit's end. I've done everything possible to attract this handsome bachelor in our church singles group. I had a facelift, breast implants, tummy and butt tucks, and a chemical peel, and people think I work at Victoria's Secret. Nothing helps. When we get together in the evening, all he wants to do is look at *Wheel of Fortune* and leer at Vanna White."

Dr. Strudel: "What a sad story. It seems you have spun the wheel and landed on bankrupt. I suggest you seek your fortune elsewhere; of the two hosts on this show, I don't think he's leering at Vanna. Who's next? The lady in red, go ahead please."

"My problem is that ever since my husband has been wearing a testosterone patch, he's horny as hell. Seafood, especially, turns him on. The other evening, after a shrimp and lobster-tail dinner, he demanded sex immediately. What do think of his behavior?"

"First of all, ma'am, a lot of women would like to have your problem. Also, seafood is healthful for the elderly. I don't feel you have a complaint."

Questioner: "Well, perhaps not. But the manager at *Red Lobster* certainly didn't see it that way. We were asked to leave, and we were barely into foreplay."

Dr. Strudel: "Ah c'mon, now, that's an old joke. We have to move along. I'll take one more question."

"Mr. Strudel, er, I'm sorry, I mean Dr. Strudel, I guess you can tell I'm a little nervous. This question doesn't concern me. It's about a friend of mine who has the flu and couldn't be here tonight. This friend was recently divorced and she is literally starved for sex. She's becoming a regular sex maniac. That's all she thinks about day and night. Sex, sex, sex!"

"Ma'am, your friend should definitely seek professional help. I'm sorry we don't have more time. Thanks again and good night. Oh, what's that, sir? Did you want to say something?"

Man in fourth row: "Yes, if the lady who asked the last question will meet me in the lobby, I would like to tell her about an excellent flu remedy which she can pass on to her friend."

12

Will Computers Write Popular Magazine Articles?

Will material in popular consumer magazines soon be written entirely by computers--without human input? I think so. I suspect it's already happening. You may wonder what's so unusual about that. Don't we already have computers that can think, interact, play championship chess, fly space ships, classify DNA, identify genes, and otherwise imitate the human brain?

That's true, but I'm not talking about using that kind of computer power. That would be like killing flies with a sledge hammer; like using atomic power to dig post holes; or sending a Huey to rescue a treed cat.

No, the kind of articles devoured by readers of most popular newsstand periodicals can be created and submitted for publication by an archaic 1982 IBM XT.

Even an old 80286, with a 10MB hard disk, could handle most jobs.

I know this because of my recent research, which anyone can easily duplicate. To wit: Ninety-five percent of all popular consumer magazine articles fall neatly into only five easily programmable categories:

1. Sex
2. Dieting
3. Health
4. Money
5. Stress

Perhaps so, you say, but each subject covers a broad spectrum of knowledge and approaches; just look at the array of cover titles: "The Surprising Secrets of Sexy Couples," "How to Keep Your Spouse From Roaming," "Mind-blowing Sex at Any Age," "Lose Ten Pounds in Ten Days," "Reduce Stress Forever," "Snack all You Want, and Still Lose," "How to Become a Millionaire and Retire at Thirty-Five," "Foods that Can Kill You," "Pills that Can Kill You," "Live to be 110."

So what's your point? Titles have nothing to do with what's in the articles, which is always the same predictable material. Each of the above five categories utilize only five sub-categories. Consider sex articles, for example. Regardless of titles--some of which would embarrass even Madonna--article content always boils down to:

1. Create romantic atmosphere.
2. Be considerate of partner's needs.

3. Avoid drugs and heavy drinking.
4. Never have sex when angry or stressed.
5. It's okay to fantasize and try new things.

So you see, to create today's magazine articles, it's just a matter of choosing one of the five major areas, with its predictable sub-categories, putting the information on a computer disk, automatically scrambling it now and then for a little variety, and, presto, you have created enough material to supply *Cosmopolitan, Redbook, McCall's, Ladies' Home Journal,* and their many clones for the next ten years. Caught on? Now let's look at the second category, dieting:

1. Keep track of calories.
2. Reduce fat intake.
3. Maintain needed nutrients.
4. Avoid snacks.
5. Get enough exercise.

Articles on health break down to:

1. Eat right.
2. Get sufficient rest.
3. Plan for recreation or hobby.
4. Exercise regularly.
5. Get periodic checkups.

Financial matters always include the following:

1. Create and follow a budget.
2. Save regularly and consistently.

3. Key all investments to your age and future plans.
4. Consider mutual funds, if cash is limited.
5. Watch credit card debt.

Finally, we come to handling stress:

1. Find cause, and try to remedy.
2. Get physical exercise.
3. Organize your life. Keep lists.
4. Learn to say no to some volunteer requests.
5. Reserve time for yourself.

There you have it. If computers take over magazine article preparation, what will editors do? Well, there are a few chores which will require their skills. Computers probably couldn't handle stories about the actress, talk show guest, or celebrity model who bears her soul on how she weathered her latest life crisis, occasioned, say, when she learned that her husband has two other wives--one of which is rumored to be a man.

Someone must handle stories on the latest celebrity "miracle baby." It has always been a source of puzzlement to me why only famous people have miracle offspring. Aren't they conceived, manufactured, and delivered in the manner of us common folk?

Also, editors will be needed to come up with those provocative titles which catch the newsstand browser's eye and sell the magazines. Look at these actual titles, promotionals, and tag lines from recent mainstream, high circulation periodicals:

"Fidelity: How Important Can it Be?" "Will Popping Pills Banish Your Blues?" "Happier, Hotter Sex," "The Health Benefits of Sex," "Make Money Even if the Market Falls," "Giving Him a Night to Remember," "Cut $1,000 From Your April 15th Taxes." And how about this one: "You're Happily Married, but Have the Hots for that Guy in the Gym. Do You Dare Fool Around?"

But, with few other opportunities to critique, rewrite, and mutilate poor writers' prose, many editors will be challenged to find new occupations in line with their emotional temperaments, experiences, and skills. Speaking as one of their long-suffering victims, I think they would do well as wrecking-ball operators in the construction industry or, perhaps, as executioners for those states that have the death penalty.

13

That's Music?

Where is Mitch Miller when we need him? Back in the fifties, when he invited everyone to sing along with him, he put lyrics on the screen, then helped us keep together with a bouncing ball over the words.

But we didn't need the words nor the ball. We understood Mitch's every word. We understood the words of almost every singer then, including Elvis. Hell, we even understood Jerry Lee Lewis. But can anyone who is old enough to remember 78 rpm records or qualify for AARP membership understand anything today's hip-hop rock and rappers are singing or saying? Now is when we sorely need the aids.

I hear that Tipper Gore understands some of the words, reporting they are not nice, so it's better we seniors remain uninformed. Names of today's groups are hardly appealing. Do we have literate names like The Lettermen, Beach Boys, Dream Weavers, or the Platters? No, we have Skinny Puppy, Superchunk, the Meat Puppets, Thrush Hermit, Snoop Doggy Dog, Gangsta Rap, and Hootie and the Blowfish.

Well, the old must give way to the new. Life, like an escalator, just keeps rolling along (or am I thinking of Old Man River?). I don't expect today's kids to dig Ray Anthony or Ray Conniff. But what some consider music now can't roll (or rock) along to something else too quickly for me.

We seniors still have our record collections and our memories of times when radio networks aired those great remotes every evening from the big ballrooms and hotels, featuring such favorites as Tommy Dorsey, Sammy Kay, Larry Clinton, Harry James, and many others direct from the Meadowbrook in Cedargrove, NJ, or perhaps the Glen Island Casino, New Rochelle, NY; the Aragon in Chicago; the Steel Pier, Atlantic City; or New York's Roseland.

Incidentally, it's shameful the way seniors are treated by the recording industry, especially when it comes to providing works of the old vocalists and choral groups. Try to find Ted Lewis, Skinnay Ennis, or Best of Fred Waring on a CD or cassette in mall stores. Ditto Kay Starr, Gracie Fields, or Six Hits and a Miss. Actually, there aren't many oldies of any kind in these outlets.

Of twenty block-long aisles of disks and tapes, nineteen are devoted to rock, rap, hip-hop, rhythm & blues, country, new age, and gospel. Finally, on aisle twenty near the end, near the floor, we find a small section labeled "Easy Listening."

There, you must stoop to read the labels. That's where you find the likes of G. Miller, T. Dorsey, V. Monroe, K. Kyser, J. Stafford, H. O'Connell, M. Whiting, T. Brewer, and others who were the last to create what reasonably is called music.

These stores should at least put these limited offerings a little higher, or else provide someone to help us oldsters up, after we develop charley horses down there while looking in vain for Gracie Fields.

14

Honest Advertising: The Ultimate Oxymoron

The hype and glitzy promises of today's advertising, compared with actual products and services delivered, leave much to be desired. Don't get me wrong. Advertising is an essential element of our economy. Without it, our lives would have to be restructured. But, hey, couldn't copywriters cruise a little closer to reality?

Some of today's advertisements are just plain stupid. Consider the scores of well-known, otherwise dignified adults who allow themselves to be featured in national publications with milk smeared across their upper lips, while asking others why they don't engage in this childish behavior.

For one thing, I don't know how they do it. I can't. The milk pours down my collar before I can get much on my upper lip, and it won't stay up there. Do they use latex paint or cake icing to create the effect? I don't know.

This campaign would have more credence if participants were asked to place their faces in a bowl of milk. The liquid would be more likely to adhere. Instead of "Where's Your Mustache?" the copy could read, "Where's Your Beard?"

"Where's Your Beard?"

How come advertisements for senior life care and retirement communities, geriatric liquid diets, sexual enhancement appliances, bladder control devices, medications, various mobility equipment--even those for retirement financial plans--always feature lively, laughing models who appear to be in their late thirties?

The youthful models in prostate medication advertisements wouldn't laugh if they, themselves, had received the "infamous finger" a couple of times. What's wrong with showing how ultimate consumers look--bald maybe, a little bent, perhaps, but proud and in control of most of their faculties, most of the time.

See the advertisements for pest control services. See the shiny fleet of specially equipped trucks shown. And, hey, get a load of the technicians, who look like something out of Star Wars. Are those electronic laser-beam silverfish eliminators in their gloved hands? I think so.

So you have a problem with ants and spiders, and you call this company. Do you get Darth Vader? No, you get a balding, dumpy little guy wearing coveralls and leather tool belt, holding a hand-pump sprayer. He only says one word when you open the door: "Exterminator."

His truck is a rusting 1985 Dodge pickup with a home-made camper shell. A bumper sticker on the back proclaims: "Save Our Nation--Shoot a Liberal." He doesn't introduce himself, but you presume his name is "Tex." Anyway, that's what it says on his big silver-tone belt buckle.

You ask Tex if he'll pay special attention to laundry room cabinets--perhaps spraying a little heavier there. Forget it. He marches to his own drummer--treats everything the same. All finished--he hands you a copy of the service order, pointing to where you should sign. Then, unlit cigar clinched firmly in his teeth, he leaves.

In all fairness to Tex, he probably did as good a job as anyone with his job description. As the old saying goes: chlorpyrifos is chlorpyrifos (I had to look that up) whether it arrives in a rusting Dodge pickup or the Starship Enterprise.

Mentally-challenged Buyers

Do you want to do business with a firm that advertises a "gigantic emergency sale" because its math-challenged buyers made a big mistake and over-ordered? Goes the copy: "Truckloads are now arriving daily, warehouses are bulging, we're hitting the panic button. If we don't raise immediate cash, Armageddon is surely at hand."

When these sales are held every month, you have to wonder why those stupid, irresponsible buyers are still there. Maybe they won't pay their suppliers, who will come to your door someday and reclaim all your purchases from that store.

Watch those "Buy" Words

Today's consumer must be wary of current fads, idioms, and politically correct terms which advertisers like to sneak in to ensnare buyers. Some don't even apply to items being touted. For example, advertisers know that products sell better if they can claim they are made of natural ingredients. I don't know what is so special about natural. Cyanide is natural. So is asbestos and uranium 235, none of which is exactly user-friendly.

Salability is also enhanced when products are made of recycled materials, are caffeine free, contain no fat, cholesterol, calories, and sodium, and will not destroy the ozone layer, rainforest, or the endangered Tasmanian goat flea. This is sometimes difficult for copywriters, especially if the product is, say, a new hemorrhoid suppository.

The "in" thing today, of course, is to claim that as much of your product as possible is made in the USA. That's why your new sneakers from Taiwan have a tag certifying that the plastic tips on the strings were made in Milwaukee, Toledo or, perhaps, Hutchinson, Kansas--by union workers.

Why do food advertisements tell us we need all kinds of unfamiliar things like antioxidants? I try to assume a positive view on most things, but if antioxidants are against oxygen, as it sounds like, I don't want any part of them.

Furthermore, I am told they have something to do with free radicals. That doesn't sound good. But, perhaps, I should keep an open mind--at least until expert nutritionists, human biologists, and medical researchers reach some kind of consensus in their own ranks.

Finally, when an advertiser claims its client's product is better than "the leading brand," did you ever wonder why the latter got to be leader in the first place, and why it's still there--rather than the one being advertised?

15

Automotive Advertising: Looking Beneath the Surface

As I grow older, I find it difficult to comprehend today's automobile advertising. I'm aware that most of it is produced by the "X" generation, but even my boomer friends say they find it puzzling. Take, for example, "Have you driven a Ford lately?" As far as I know, Fords have always enjoyed a fairly good reputation for quality. But their slogan implies that while their cars were bad for awhile, they're better now. So try us again.

The Cadillac that Zigs?

General Motors claims that its Catera is the Cadillac that zigs. Does it also zag, as in zigzag? Does this car have a steering problem? Dealers deny it. Salespersons who were questioned said they didn't know what "zigs" means. Anthologies having to do with word origins provide little help.

However, any veteran who served in Europe during World War II can provide as good a definition as any--authenticated by at least five dictionaries of slang. Then, zig or zig-zig was universally understood as an invitation to make whoopee--a proposition, so to speak, resulting (if the initiator were lucky) in zigging. So how, who, or what does the Catera zig? I don't know. But until I get more information, I'm not going to park my Toyota Tercel near one after dark.

Marilyn Monroe and Sheet Metal

In one of the decade's more cryptic (and expensive) automotive magazine advertisements, Mercedes presents a full-page, full-color portrait of the late Marilyn Monroe. Near the bottom is only one word--Glamour. That's it! The only clue to the sponsor is a beauty spot on Marilyn's cheek. A magnifying glass reveals a tiny Mercedes hood ornament.

Glamour indeed. The company couldn't have found a more suitable persona with which to compare its styling. But beauty and sheet metal are only skin deep. I can't help but recall some of Ms. Monroe's less desirable traits. It is well known that she was unstable, unreliable, and undependable--traits you don't want associated with an automobile.

Why Do Writers Rate Cars?

Why do automotive magazines rate new cars each year, naming their favorite "Car of the Year?" That honor becomes the basis for that maker's advertising. What do writers and editors know about mechanics? They went to

journalism school--if they went to school at all. Why not have an independent panel of automotive experts determine which new set of wheels is best?

The panel should consist of an automotive engineer from each of the Big Three and Toyota (to give it class), two New York taxi drivers, a couple of high school seniors (preferably jocks), and one or two "shade-tree mechanics," preferably from somewhere in Tennessee. Let this group drive 'em all, and you'll get honest and meaningful data.

Auto Advertising for the Technically-deprived

I hate advertisements that try to snow the consumer with high-sounding technical terms, which copywriters know no one understands. They don't understand them. Take "rack and pinion" steering, for example, mentioned in many automotive advertisements. Steering I know about. Why can't they just say: "If you are sober, you can depend on our steering to keep you in your lane."

But when I see **rack and pinion,** I envision some poor bastard stretched out on a rack in a medieval dungeon, screaming in agony as his bones, muscles, and tendons slowly become disjointed, and who is about to receive the coup de grace with a pinion. I'm not quite sure what a pinion is, but I think it was used during the Spanish Inquisition, or perhaps even as early as the Sacking of Rome in 1527. I want steering with a more humane connotation.

Look at tire advertisements. A company advertises a new tire for $23.95*. The asterisk indicates that costs are higher for some tires. So I check out this apparent bargain, only to find out that the advertised tire is only for the 1954 Nash Metropolitan. Treads for my car, I was told, would be $65 each.

To digress a moment--when I bought my first new car back in 1947, I expected to run the tires about 15,000 miles before they resembled the surface of bowling balls. That's the way they made them then. The product has been improved considerably in the last half-century. For one thing, we don't need tubes, and don't have to carry hot-patch kits, but tire advertising has changed little.

Back to the present: I needed four new tires, so I told the dealer to put 'em on. Let's see, 4 x 65 is $260, plus 6% state tax--I should be able to buy new rubber for $270.60. Right? Why then did I have to pay $325 when I picked up my car? The affable young woman at the cashier's window was more than happy to explain.

"First," she said, "there's the mounting charge. It isn't included on this special. Then there's electronic balancing and weights, road hazard insurance, which I'm sure you want, road testing, and, of course, the fee for the old tire disposal fund. That's the law, you know," she concluded.

Well, I certainly know now. As I understand it, my old tires have a secure, comfortable hospice in which to spend their final days, while I can't even afford nursing home insurance. It's my fault, of course, for not reading disclaimers at the bottom of the advertisement, but I didn't have a 10x magnifying glass.

Woe to those who try to read disclaimers on television commercials, especially those for automotive leases. They're carefully timed to appear for no more than a giga-second in 3-point type. If they appeared longer, you would discover that the attractive $539 a month lease on a new foreign luxury sedan, featured in the bold headline, is available only after making a pre-payment of $5,000, plus deed to your home, and ten months of involuntary servitude.

16

Advertising: A Few Good Words

In all fairness, I must mention some of advertising's positive attributes. In this age of synthetics and substitutions, we need copywriters and packaging designers to tell us that what we are buying is really what we think we are buying. Some of them do.

For example, the package for Swanson's Veal Parmigiana proclaims in bold letters: **Made with Real Veal**. That information was a real help to me. I always thought veal parmigiana was made with real pork bellies.

I would like to salute the creative advertising geniuses who came up with that great promotion for Coca-Cola. Who else could persuade consumers to pay Coke (as opposed to vice-versa) for the privilege of advertising its products on their clothing, sports equipment, toys, and scores of other products?

The Rebirth of Baking Soda

Consider what advertising has done for lowly baking soda. Forty years ago, this product was used mostly for baking, in mostly rural areas. Also, some people took it for upset stomach, or applied it as a soothing emollient for wasp stings.

I used to pity one of my aunts because she brushed her teeth with baking soda. I just figured she couldn't afford Ipana or Colgate. At age 86, she still had all her teeth. When people stopped baking at home, soda limped along for years mainly as a refrigerator deodorant.

Now, thanks to advertising's big heart, and mass marketing, it's the most publicized ingredient in the health and beauty field. It's found in toothpaste, mouthwash, deodorant, carpet cleaner, cat litter, and on and on. It's also the secret ingredient in Rogaine. Not.

Bringing Back Denim

Observe what advertising has done for once humble blue jeans. When I was a kid, I would have been ashamed to wear a pair to school. Poor kid, everyone would have said. Must live on the other side of the tracks. This appraisal would have been uttered even more fervently if the jeans were badly worn, ripped, or patched. Now such tortured threads are flaunted by debutantes.

I did wear jeans on Saturday, when forced to clean the basement or garage under threat of not going to the Saturday matinee. I knew Tom Mix, Hoot Gibson, and Gabby Hayes wore jeans. But those were in movies made in foreign lands like New Mexico and Arizona, where they also wore gun belts, chaps, spurs, and ten-gallon hats. You didn't wear those things to grammar school either.

My uncle, a Midwest farmer, used to keep a denim jacket in the barn to wear when he shoveled manure out of cattle stalls. He bought it new for $3, right after World War II. Worn thin in places, it served its purpose well for many years.

That was before Jordache, Z. Cavaricci, and Gloria Vanderbilt got into the act. Recently, when a tour bus I was on stopped on Beverly Hill's Rodeo Drive, I saw nearly the same denim jacket as my uncle's at a sidewalk sale, brass buttons and all--even had stressed elbows. The tag said $165.

To paraphrase a popular slogan, "We've come a long way, baby." Advertising had a lot to do with getting us here. But on a road that's never smooth, couldn't it avoid some of the potholes?

17

Politically Correct Tipping

Everyone is familiar with customs involved in the everyday practice of proffering gratuities, although they differ on proper amounts. Eligible recipients include those associated with dining, health clubs, travel, valet parking, barber shops, and beauty salons. Then, during the winter holidays, hands reach out from every direction--some of which we don't recognize.

The media run articles outlining suggested amounts for such service providers as post person, garbage person, newspaper delivery person, maid, gardener, doorman, bus driver, building superintendent, and garage attendant. You're also reminded that year-round tippees, mentioned at the beginning, are to be remembered with special gifts.

Never mind that the garbage person, a member of the Teamsters, earns twenty thousand a year more than you, ditto the postperson. Forget that the newspaper delivery person tosses your daily into your shrubbery from the window of his new Buick Riviera, and you drive a '92 Ford Taurus. Custom is custom, and custom must be preserved.

It is my opinion that tipping only those popularly perceived to be at the low end of the service spectrum is discrimination in its ugliest sense. It's like, yea worse, than holding a door for your female secretary, when you don't hold doors for your male associates.

The Hoi Polloi

You're discriminating (sexual discrimination) because you have placed her in a special category. Limiting our handouts to only manual laborers, for example, is saying, "You're strictly hoi polloi--a caste below us. So hold out your hats and we'll toss in a few bills."

If you are politically correct today (and it's politically correct so to be), you can't discriminate in your giving. It's cut it out altogether, or include all those who have served you. For example, what about your doctor?

For your family physician, a hundred dollars is probably sufficient, along with, say, fifty for his nurse, and twenty-five for the receptionist. A specialist deserves more, depending on what he has done.

If he only said "Hmmmm" a couple of times when looking at your records, a hundred and fifty should suffice. But if he actually spent the entire seven minutes with you (the standard patient-time allotment for many specialties), a little more is in line.

Don't forget your dentist, dental hygienist, tax accountant, broker, and bookie. In the case of the last three, give unto each as they have given unto you. And who is more deserving than members of your city government? The mayor and council members serve you three hundred and sixty-five days a year, with no thoughts of themselves or of personal gain.

They're all heart, these public servants, and each deserves at least a bottle of Chivas Regal, Courvoisier Cognac or, perhaps, a magnum of Taittinger's. If you run into money troubles, remember your friendly banker is always there for you.

In addition to interest withheld on your loan, it would not be out of line to flip your fiduciary angel an extra twenty, and don't forget his secretary, and the guard at the door who protects your deposits and safe deposit box all year long.

Time for Mistletoe and Tipping

The winter holidays are the season of tipping, the season of joy, tipping, sugar plumbs, tipping, silver bells, tipping, reindeer, mistletoe, egg nog, jolly Santas, twinkling lights, tipping, goodwill toward persons, and tipping--politically correct tipping.

Don't blame me. I had nothing to do with this political correctness thing. But you can thank me for bringing this matter to your attention, and reminding you that, if you tip your barber and not your broker, you're insulting the former and discriminating against the latter.

18

Designer Water: Where Will It End?

I would like to say right off that, as one who is on the north side of seventy, I am both a fan and avid consumer of bottled water. It's healthful, convenient and, among its other attributes, is necessary for safe foreign travel. But I find amusing the excessive hoopla, sophistry, and general savoir-faire being accorded this essential-for-life product.

Not just any pure water can be bottled anymore. It must come from "long-hidden primal springs," "sparkling mountain streams high in the Himalayas," or, perhaps, "ancient glaciers." The more distant and remote the source, the greater the mystique (and price).

It comes in liter and half-liter bottles, with attractive, environmentally-friendly labels featuring pictures of fawns, roaring streams, and snow-capped peaks. It's sold in supermarkets, bars, and trendy boutiques for nearly a hundred times the cost of equivalent tap water.

Some products, because of their fancy labels and higher prices, are termed mod or designer waters. Next to driving a 4X4, having sexy ABS, and an E-mail address, drinking mod water is about as "with it" as you can get.

Legend has it a Frenchman, back in 1798, was the first to sell bottled water, which came from a spring near his home. His name couldn't be verified, but since he was French, we'll call him Henri. When Henri announced his plans, he must have had to endure a lot of ribbing, A likely scenario:

A bistro buddy speaks, "Money for bottled wine, yes. But water? What Frenchman drinks water?"

Says another, "Hey, guys, look what Crazy Henri is up to now," as he describes Henri's new project. Henri's face quickly resembles vin rouge, as others in the group elbow each other and hold their stomachs to stifle laughter. "What's next, mon ami? Are you going to bottle and sell air?"

Suggests still another, "When the moon hangs low over the Pyrénées, perhaps he will catch and package moonbeams. Oui? Ah, poor Henri. If he thinks people will pay money for plain water in little bottles, I would like to show him a bridge in Paris I have for sale." Now the entire group doubles over in uncontrolled frivolity.

If Henri were around today, he would have the last laugh. According to the International Bottled Water Association (IBWA), Americans shell out more than $3.7 billion annually for flat bottled water (as opposed to carbonated variety), with some 700 domestic and foreign producers supplying their needs.

Bottled water has reached celebrity status only during the last decade or so. It's what's on the bottle, not what's in it, that counts. Hakeem Olajuwon, Houston Rockets star center and 1994 NBA MVP, recently introduced Hakeem Olajuwon H_2O in the Houston area, complete with his picture on the label. He hopes to go national with his brand (no fair, basketball fans, please don't refill "The Dream's" designer bottle from the tap).

New York designer Donna Karan put her popular DKNY label on bottled water several years ago, as part of a special promotion. Although currently not being sold, it made quite a splash with the Rodeo Drive crowd, especially when ensconced in a chic, custom carrier by Chanel (now, Mrs. Van Uppington, you shouldn't pour Safeway-brand water into the empty DKNY bottle).

Fashionable department store chain, Nordstrom, offers "Nordstrom Water," at a pricey $2.50 per liter. The product is touted as having a different molecular structure than regular water, which some claim slows the aging process. Have they finally discovered the fountain of youth?

I believe this trend will continue. Where are you Liz, Max Factor, and LA Gear? For those who wish to switch from colas to water, but fear giving up their daily jolt of caffeine, there are now some twelve companies producing caffeine-laced bottled water, according to a recent article in *USA Today*.

I suppose it had to happen; bottled water is going to the dogs (and cats), and is found in supermarkets and pet stores across the country. I don't think my Weimaraner, Earl, would be impressed. He's a downright, down-to-earth critter. We make his day when we leave home and forget to put the toilet lid down.

But future producers of bottled water for dogs would do well to cater to the likes of Earl. He won't go for some hotsie-totsie brand, designed primarily to impress French poodles. Labels like Bird Bath, Commode, and Muddy Puddle would be more to his liking. Subtle flavors, say, essence of house slipper, road kill, and carrion could be added. Earl would wax ecstatic at the scent of any of those.

But designer water for Earl wouldn't be cost-effective. You see, Earl's jowls are somewhat pelican-like in their ability to hold liquids. When he leaves his water bowl, the trail he leaves across the kitchen floor is generally equal (sometimes greater) to what he drank.

I hope our cat, Ethel, never finds out about bottled cat water! She's been hard to get along with ever since she saw that uppity feline on TV--the one that eats from a crystal bowl. Forgetting we found her behind Arby's one cold night only three months ago, shivering and hungry, Ethel now refuses to eat out of anything except my wife's Waterford. So much for gratitude.

What's ahead? Will we soon have bottled water for birds and fish? How about designer water for house plants? Don't laugh. IBWA's director of communication, Jennifer Levine, says she knows people who are already pouring bottled water over their prized specimens. I hope this trend doesn't get out of hand. Orchids will want DKNY.

19

Elder Fraud and other Myths

The stories differ only in the details: Trusting, white-haired seniors lose life savings to "boiler room" telephone scams or door-to-door flimflam artists. How pitiful. Well, call me hard-hearted, but I don't think the common-sense lobe of the brain disappears on one's sixty-fifth birthday.

Those who are fooled and robbed of their resources during their golden years, would have been duped just as easily when they were twenty-five. Age has nothing to do with gullibility--the attribute to be pitied. It's usually the "free lunch" pitch that snares most victims. By the time they are seniors, they should have learned there ain't no such thing.

Okay, enough sermon. Do I get calls or letters from strangers who want to share their wealth with me because of their great love for humanity, and for me in particular? Yes, about two or three a week. I've turned these contacts into a participative sport. After all, I don't play golf or tennis. I'm entitled to a little fun.

Recently, I received an "official" letter, bearing all kinds of seals and signatures from important-sounding people, informing me I may have won a new Buick or other valuable prize. The sender wanted to know what color car I would like, and requested a "final verification and confirmation fee" of only $15.00. Visa or MasterCard welcome.

I didn't send the $15.00. For such generosity, I felt they deserved more. So I sent them the "free Bahamas vacation" certificate which another generous stranger gave me. It's reportedly worth $500. I told them to keep the change, and to send me a blue Buick. To redeem the certificate, they'll only have to pay a small "verification and confirmation fee," plus all airfare, lodging, and meals during their "free" vacation.

Helping Ed and Dick

Of course, there are legitimate sweepstakes, which ask only that you subscribe to their magazines. Publishers Clearing House comes to mind. I think we should help that hard-working pair, Ed McMahon and Dick Clark, whenever we can. After all, they're golden agers just like us.

But are they taking it easy? Have they joined the shuffleboard set? No! They're down at the office every day, sending out those messages of hope, telling us they could arrive at our front door soon with that once-in-a-lifetime, whopping supplement to our Social Security income.

Ed and Dick themselves can't participate in this promotion. That's why, when I receive a notice from *Reader's Digest,* saying I'm a "finalist" in its sweeps, I unselfishly write their names on the reply card, and return it to the *Digest* promotion. I even send them the gold rub-off card and magic sticker. I hope they win. They deserve it.

Telephone Solicitors

But telephone solicitors provide the most amusement, especially since I've learned to handle them. Such calls used to go something like this: "Hello George, how are you tonight?" So downright friendly, and calls me by my first name, surely I must know this person. Perhaps an old army or college buddy.

So I reply, "I'm fine," which was the wrong thing to say. My caller says he's happy to hear that, and he knows I'm someone who would like to help others to feel fine, too. My gift of only $25.00, sent to a box number, would enable ten disadvantaged children to attend the circus.

When I reply that the circus just left our city last week and won't return for a year, he becomes a bit surly. "Okay, so we'll take them to the movies. Just send the money, or give us your VISA card number." We don't part cordially. Now, I have learned to never let these callers get past asking, "How you are tonight?"

When they begin with that question (and they always do), I reply, "It's so nice of you to inquire. I'm not at all well. My hemorrhoids are acting up again. Pain. Itch. It's enough to drive ya nuts. Then, I've had this bad cold for the past month. Can't seem to shake it. My kidney condition is back. Have to get up two or three times a night. Believe me, that's no fun. No fun at all.

"On top of everything else, the doc says I need a gall bladder operation. Got a call from my cousin the other day. He went on for ten minutes about his toenail fungus. I told him he was lucky; he oughta have my problems. Well, I'm sure you didn't call to inquire about my cousin. After all, you asked how I am, and I appreciate it. I'd also like to tell you about this ringing in my ears and, and the shooting pain in my... Hello. HELLO. Are you there?" (dial tone). Works every time.

My approach is also effective with the bond salesman from Smith Barney, and the woman from AT&T who calls every night to try to lure me back from MCI. I switched once. Then the guy from MCI called every night. Some well-meaning people defend telemarketers by saying, "Everyone has a right to make a living." True, but the same argument could be used to defend mosquitoes.

20

The Retired Male as Chef

An old vaudeville joke goes something like this: Wife to husband: "Fred, next door, kisses his wife ten times every day. Why don't you do that?" Husband: "I'd like to, but I don't think Fred would like it."

Well, it's easy to see why that genre died a long time ago. Nevertheless, I should have been ready with a similarly effective retort when my wife mentioned recently that her friend Jane was teaching her retired husband to cook, and since I was now a member of that leisure class, perhaps...well, you can imagine the rest.

I knew I should have joined the neighborhood woodworking club, volunteered at the hospital, or even signed up for an adult education class at the university. At least I would have studied something useful, like fly tying.

But now it was too late. I was destined to sweat over a hot stove all day.

Under good wife's expert instruction, I was doing well in my first culinary course--Pasta 101. I had just begun dropping the vermicelli into boiling water, when my teacher received a telephone call. She was on for some time, so I decided to surprise her with a finished meal. What a snap, I thought. I opened wine, made garlic bread, got out her best linen napkins, and put on a dreamy Dean Martin disc. When I heard her coming, I yelled, "Surprise! Surprise! Prepare to imagine you're in old Napoli!"

"Why are you serving the vermicelli in those large bowls?" she inquired.

"Well," I replied proudly, "it seems a little thin for plates."

"Oh no!" she cried. "Oh no! No! No! You're supposed to drain off the boiling water BEFORE adding the sauce."

For a moment, I suffered a flashback to my high school days, remembering when I had laughed at boys who took home economics. I wouldn't laugh now. I was fully subdued. I had flunked my first lesson. There were other dark periods, of course. Like the time I totaled the microwave while trying to cook eggs in the shell. But I'm catching on to this chef thing--even enjoying it.

Recent guests raved over my jalapeno-Jello mold. They sat there with open mouths. Ditto my sweet-sour eggplant and, on another occasion, my improved eggs Benedict, which I call eggs-Benedictine (you substitute a shot of B&B for hollandaise sauce).

Why is cooking such a big deal? Many of its archaic practices could benefit from modern technology. I'll do what I can. Microwave oven manufacturers, as well as TV dinner makers, should welcome my idea on how to better utilize their products.

Some TV dinners have rather involved preparation instructions. "Heat on high for five minutes, then switch to fifty percent power for ten minutes, then let set for a minute." Or something like that.

In addition, instructions are often printed on the bottom of the the tray, which you discover only after removing the top. Turn it over now, and you spill the entire contents. Holding it high above your head, as you gaze upward, might cause you to lose your balance.

The solution: Learn from the VCR***plus***+ people. Put a distinctive code number on top of every package. Place TV dinner in oven, and key in the number. Oven will provide the correct power for each cooking stage and deliver a finished meal. Damn, I surprise myself at times!

I have other brilliant ideas of this ilk, not all of which I can reveal here for proprietary reasons. But, suffice it to say, I think great things are ahead for my biodegradable, throw-away, grease-absorbing, skillet cover liner--indispensable in preparing liver and onions. When liner is fully saturated, replace, and throw old one in your kitchen compost container.

I have also drawn up plans for a vacuum hose attachment for the garbage disposal. It permits a quick sink and counter cleanup, but also handily disposes of items any good cook--such as myself--drops on the floor, like pickle slices, flour, egg yokes, dollops of sour cream, whatever.

Incidentally, I would like to point out what I feel has been a TV dinner industry oversight. You're always told to uncover applesauce, pudding, or other dessert, but punch holes over other items. But the dessert is placed in the middle. You can't uncover it without uncovering everything else. Solution: Put dessert in a corner.

With a little more time, research, and experimentation, I'm sure I can bring this cooking thing into the twenty-first century. My wife is certainly pleased with my progress. I know this by the nice little things she does for me. Just this week, she presented me with a one-year membership in the woodworking club.

Excuse me, there's the doorbell. It was Jane's husband. He wanted to know if I would like to join him as a volunteer at the senior day-care center. It seems our wives discussed this and agreed it's a great activity for both of us. Hey, come to think of it, we can assist the dietician and cooks with the center's food and nutrition program. They'll appreciate that.

21

The Computer Revolution: Please Don't Turn so Fast

I've been developing this disorder for some time. So it isn't that I didn't expect it, but that doesn't ease the pain. I have Computer Obsolescence Depression (COD). Perhaps you've heard of it. Various forms are known as Multimedia Melancholia (MM), Cybernetic Cynicism (CC), Internet Inertia (II), Digital Deprivation (DD), Pentium Pensiveness (PP), and Windows 95 Withdrawal (W95W).

Actually, I noticed the first minor symptoms about 30 years ago, at about the time our friends were getting color television sets. We still had a primitive 18-inch b&w Hoffman. But since it had a green-tinted, anti-glare screen, it looked a little like a color receiver when off, and we were careful never to turn it on when guests dropped in.

We would have kept it much longer if the corner drug store hadn't taken out its vacuum tube tester. We eventually got a color receiver--one that not only worked exceptionally well, but also was "socially acceptable" for more than two decades. We expect our current TV to last as long.

The planned obsolescence gurus in Silicon Valley, who have a new computer on the market before you can get home with one you've just purchased, could learn a lot from the TV industry. A PC purchased today will undoubtedly work well for twenty years, too, but what would the neighbors and your golfing buddies think?

First on the Block

No longer suffering from television denial and its attendant shame, I staged a real neighborhood coup. The year was 1984, and I was the first on our block to buy a personal computer (PC). What a beauty--an IBM 80286 with 640K RAM, a ten megabyte hard disk (yes, they made them that small), and two 5.25-inch floppy disk drives.

I never quite figured out why I purchased two, since I had a hard disk, but the computer at the company where I worked had only one, and now I had two. That seemed to put me in the vanguard. Complete outfit, including monochrome monitor, a modem I never learned to use, daisy-wheel printer, and an early version of WordStar, ran a little over $3,000.

I thought I would keep it forever. Never mind its street value was less than $800 barely ten months later. It was mine, and I loved it like a brother. Neighbors were impressed, too--for a while. They used to bring their out-of-town visitors over to see it, always cautioning them not to stand too close in case of fallout.

Eager students watch demonstration of an early computer. Is that young Bill Gates (standing at right)? Probably not.

The 80286 and I got along fine for about five years, or until my daughter and son-in-law came for a visit. I showed them my computer, demonstrated what it did, then leaned back in anticipation of their expressions of awe. Their only response was to exchange pitying glances. Better had I showed them my prized tomato plants.

My son-in-law spoke first: "Dad, we don't want to hurt your feelings, but you've got a real brontosaurus there. Pretty soon, people will talk."

"We'll help bring you into the twenty-first century," said my daughter, a tear glistening in her eye as she placed a loving, understanding hand on my shoulder. "Tomorrow, we're going computer shopping."

That's how I became owner of my present setup--a 80386/33MHz processor with 8MB RAM, a color graphics monitor, 200MB hard disk, laser printer, Windows, WordPerfect, and a VISA card on which the credit limit was extended. That was several years ago, and I don't care what the street value of my equipment is now. It works for me.

I'm not against progress, but I prefer it in moderate doses. I have gone as far as I'm going for a long time. Before I buy another piece of equipment, I've promised myself I'll complete two major projects of equal magnitude. Finish *War and Peace,* and read the factory-supplied DOS (disk operating system) manual all the way through. That will take awhile.

But forces of stigma and admonishment, cleverly disguised and clothed in the garments of progress, keep manifesting themselves in myriad ways. Their voices cry out: lead or move out of the way; use it or lose it; even, don't live in Jurassic Park.

I ignore them all. So far I have resisted pressures to buy a Pentium CPU. I have turned my back on CD-ROMs, and spurned the advances of multi-media. I prefer "real" reality to the virtual variety. I'll leave nets to butterflies, and webs to spiders.

But sometimes, I'm reminded in subtle ways that I travel on unpaved country lanes, while others whiz by on information superhighways. For example, I recently suffered a minor CC relapse when our minister announced we can now bring our spiritual concerns to him via E-mail. He also invited us to visit him at his web site.

Mouths of Babes

And take the other day when Jimmy, a five-year-old neighbor boy, stopped by our house after kindergarten for some of my wife's fresh-baked cookies and a glass of milk.

"Can I watch you work at your computer?" he asked.

"If you'll wash your hands, keep your milk and cookies on the table behind me, and don't talk to me," I replied. "If you get bored, read a comic book." All went well until I felt a tap on my shoulder.

"What is it, Jimmy?" I acknowledged. "Would you like more cookies?"

"No, thanks, I have plenty," he said. "But I think I should tell you that if you're trying to copy that highlighted block to a new document, you'll have to establish the file first. Maybe you meant to put it in an existing file. If so, just hit Alt, and the F4 key, and try again. Also, if you'll use a macro for your address, you can save a lot of keystrokes," he concluded. So much for milk and cookies.

There are other reminders, of course. Some of which are not too subtle. "Getting prepared to surf the net, eh man?" queried the clerk in the computer store where I was browsing through software the other day, while waiting for my wife to finish shopping next door. "Gonna cruise down that information fast lane, right?"

"No, man," I replied, trying also to be cool or hep or whatever it is they are these days. "I'm quite content to surf the card catalog at the library for information." His expression, as he brushed back his pony-tail and adjusted his earrings, indicated he wasn't cool or hep when it came to libraries.

The plumber, called to fix our kitchen disposal, after asking if I had a computer, proceeded to make an unsolicited appraisal of its capabilities or lack thereof. My COD took a turn for the worse and I even suffered a few pangs of DD, as he said, "I guess it's okay for some things. Beats the old typewriter, anyway, right?

"You should see the setup I got in my game room," he continued. "It's a 90MHz Pentium with a 4x CD-ROM, 60 watt stereo-monitor speakers, and a 48 watt subwoofer that'll blow you right outa the room," he said, pounding the kitchen cabinet for emphasis.

Is there any relief in sight for those who suffer from COD and its associated maladies? No, not unless IBM, Apple, Bill Gates and Microsoft, and other major pushers are reined in, as well as their suppliers, like Texas

Instruments and Intel, the latter being a big inside operator (a little computer humor there).

In the meantime, we sufferers must seek balm for our wounds and remedies for our pains wherever we can. Next week, Sam, an electrician I've known for many years, is coming to install a couple of additional 110v outlets in the room where I have my computer. He takes great pride in staying on the leading edge of digital technology. Worse yet, he loves to talk about it.

Sam's computer room is easily mistaken for NASA Control. His neighbors still bring their out-of-town visitors over to see his setup. I'm no match for Sam in the digital arena, and I'm tired of being the 98-kilobyte weakling who always gets silicon kicked in his face. So I'm going to do the only prudent thing--throw a blanket over my PC before he comes. Perhaps he'll think it's a sewing machine, and not ask any questions.

22

Push "F" for Frustration

Ace Computer Supply (not its real name) has a fine reputation for service and reliability. At least that was true until recently. A year ago, a call to Ace went something like this:

"Ace Computer. Nellie speaking. How can I help you?"

"Good morning, Nellie. I'd like to speak to Roy in shipping, please."

"Certainly. One moment, please."

"Yo, shipping, Roy here."

"Hey Roy, how ya doin'? This is George in Philadelphia. Just wanted to see if my back-ordered part came in."

"Hey, buddy. Good to hear from you. Do you have the original invoice number handy?"

"Yeah, it's OC-89642."

"Gotcha. Let me check my file. Okay, it's in. Came this morning. I'll ship it UPS tonight."

"Thanks, Roy. I knew I could count on you."

The total time for such an exchange was three and a half minutes. But, alas, that was before Ace Computer installed a completely automated call processing system, in order to "facilitate" such transactions.

A recent call to check on a back-ordered item went like this:

"Good morning, Ace Computer," cooed a digitized voice in full, measured tones. "If you have a touch-tone phone, press (l) now. If you are calling from a rotary phone, remain on the line for an operator."

I press (1). (Incidentally, I learned later that Nellie was out-placed shortly after the new system was installed. The old-fashioned designation for this procedure was called "getting the ax.")

"Thank you," continued the programmed voice. "Please listen carefully to the following eight-part menu. You may press the desired number at any time. Should you wish to have the menu repeated, press the (#) sign.

"Sales and marketing, press (1); Consumer affairs, press (2); Operations, press (3); Shipping and Receiving, press (4). If you would like..." Hey, (4) that's for me--I think. **I jam my finger into (4).**

(4) Answers. "Thank you for calling shipping and receiving. You may make your selection at any time from the following five-part menu: If you are a distributor, press (1); if you are a retailer, press (2); if you ordered from our catalog, press (3). if you..." **I press (3).**

(3) Answers. "If this concerns a complete shipment, press (1); an incomplete or back-ordered shipment, press (2); If you are inquiring..." **I hurriedly press (2).**

(2) Answers. "Welcome to our new fully automated back-ordered merchandise system. For quick, efficient service, please select from the following menu: For orders placed prior to December 31, press (1); for all subsequent orders, press (2)." **I press (2).**

(2) Answers. "If your name begins with A - K, press (1); L - R, press (2); S - Z, press (3)." **I press (1).**

(1) Answers. "Please enter your complete invoice number, followed by the # sign." I'm ready for 'em. I enter the number, plus #.

Computer voice: "That file doesn't come up. If you would like to speak to a supervisor, push the # sign followed by the * sign." **I enter #*.**

Recorded voice answers: "All of our representatives are busy with other customers right now, but your call is important to us. Please hold, we'll be with you in a moment." (Music for next five minutes). I was never really fond of Franz Liszt, but I suppose I can bear with a few strains of <u>Dance of the Gnomes</u> again, if it helps my cause.

"Our representatives are still busy...still busy...still busy...still busy. Thanks for holding...holding, holding, holding. Your call is important to us...to us...to us..." Ah, finally, a ring. "Hello. This is Tom Williams in back-order tracing. I'm not at my desk right now, but if you would like to leave a message, please start speaking after the beep."

Beep. "Thank you, Mr. Williams, I would like to inquire about" (another computer voice interrupts) "I'm sorry, that voice mail box is full. Please try again later. Thank you. Goodbye." **Dial-tone**.

For those who have experienced it, there is no greater or more profound sense of finality, loss, and total abandonment, than that experienced when one is told goodbye by a machine, and left with no further recourse.

What did I do? Simple. I pretended I had a rotary phone. When the live voice came in, I asked for Roy in shipping. I was happy to learn he hadn't been out-placed.

23

Today's Business: Viewing with Alarm

I have been retired from the business world for several years now. Not encumbered with day-to-day distractions and annoyances, I'm able to see things more clearly than those still directly involved. You gain that perspective, vision, and confidence as the years pass. Accordingly, I note some disturbing trends, and feel it my duty to apprize those affected before it's too late.

First, there is a not-so-hidden campaign going on to defame the office cubicle. The highly visible perpetrator of this devious endeavor is one Scott Adams, creator of a character called Dilbert. There is little doubt that Dilbert and his ilk are out to poison the minds of employees who are too young to remember the office from hell before cubicles.

That office was called the bull pen, the land-based equivalent of steerage. Employees toiled at row upon row of tightly jammed steel desks under glaring overhead lights. You had to go to the end of the row to get out. There was no place to put your coat, hang a scenic calendar, or display your Empire State Building souvenir snow globe.

One person's sneeze contaminated two hundred others. Long business calls were always suspect. Were you really talking with your Aunt Millie in Milwaukee? And the resultant fetor of anonymous flatulence caused everyone in the affected area to avoid eye contact for at least ten minutes.

Cubicles provide privacy, promote dignity, and help increase self-esteem, to say nothing of increased productivity. Many of today's enclosures provide soundproofing, individual task lighting, and air quality control. Call off your cadre of cubicle cutthroats, Mr. Scott, before you return our nation's offices to the dark ages.

Don't Move Up to Dress Down

A good idea that took root while I was still working is now being threatened by various commercial interests. I'm talking about "dress-down day," usually observed on Friday. Employees, from boss on down, are encouraged to dress casually. Jeans and tee-shirts are fine as long as they're clean and in good repair. The original concept was to promote a relaxed, informal atmosphere to improve employee relations--just as long as the work got done, and customers were not affected. That was fair.

Things worked out well for awhile. Getting some use out of your old clothes was a plus. Then the likes of Ralph Lauren, Donna Karan, Guess, Calvin Klein, Liz Claiborne, and Donna Ricco got wind of the trend.

"Hey, we're missing out on something big here," they cried, almost in unison. "Clearly, dress-down designer duds are in order." Now, if the casual clothes you wear on Friday don't cost more than the Brooks Brothers attire you wore on Thursday, you stand to be labeled a non-team player. It's time for employees to stand up and demand to dress down, in accordance with the true spirit of the day.

Don't Discard Ladder

According to current businessmagazines, corporate ladders no longer exist. Trying to go straight up is no way to get to the top, say experts. Instead, you should go outward--broaden your knowledge, skills, contacts, and information sources.

Forget about titles and promotions, croon the gurus. The "in-thing" today is the project team. Furthermore, according to a writer in a recent issue of *Fortune,* players must be skilled in "cross-functional collaboration." No longer try to become an expert in one field. Become a self-contained, multi-skilled entity, ready to join any team anywhere (even in another company) at a moment's notice, conclude the business soothsayers.

Nonsense. Consultants and business school professors come up with this kind of stuff periodically because, well, it's what they do. Broadening is okay, but don't become so horizontally structured you don't look up once in a while. You could fail to notice those who never did away with ladders in the first place--just kept them hidden until an opportune time. They could be nearing the upper rungs.

Easing the Transition

The fast trip from business world to retirement isn't easy, as thousands who have experienced it during the past decade--many prematurely--can attest. But it's inevitable. One day you're identified with your job. The next day, you're stripped of your rank and drummed out of the corps, cast into the desert with a broken sword or, perhaps more appropriately, a tarnished Cross pen and empty carafe.

Even during these days of mass downsizings, businesses should do more to ease this passage of their faithful. It is not within the scope of this treatise to say exactly what, but I would like to make one suggestion: Please redesign the cover illustrations on retirement manuals.

They're still the same as they were in the glory days of upward growth. Depicted, for example, is a contented couple lounging beside a pool behind their villa, as they enjoy a long-cool-one. Sometimes, one or the other reclines in a hammock. A tennis racket or golf bag is placed casually to one side.

On some manual covers, the couple is playing shuffleboard, while their friends prepare a barbecue. I have never known a couple who spent their retirement years playing shuffleboard. Of course, that doesn't mean they aren't out there. Regardless, captions always read:

"Your company wants you to enjoy your golden years, free from financial worries."

What an intriguing fantasy--a real fun statement. But, unless you were one of the lucky few who benefitted from stock options or buy-outs, your total monthly pension is probably equal to what it cost to fill the pool in the first illustration. These manuals should depict retirement more realistically. How about showing a retiree working as a greeter at Wal-Mart?

24

The Perils and Pleasures of Warehouse Shopping

The home-owned neighborhood hardware store, stationer, grocery, variety, and clothing stores, were warm, friendly, helpful places. Their owners lived in the community. You parked in front of their stores. The clerks knew you, asked about your family, and went out of their way to provide service.

"You want eight screws, three bolts, and six washers? Sure. Would you like that pipe cut and threaded? No problem. Say hello to your wife (husband). See you at the high school football game Saturday."

The scene has changed. Enter the big warehouse stores which, for one advanced in years, are about as much fun to shop as a rash in your private parts. They cover (the stores, not the rash) two square blocks, and with few exceptions, sell only one category of merchandise.

One sells hardware, another office supplies, still another linens, or food, or computers, or pet supplies, or toys. Parking lots extend to the horizon with no spaces open. I recently saw a mall store which sold only kites. Is a kite discount warehouse far off?

To get a few screws or washers, you must buy two dozen in a plastic bubble pack, which requires a hack saw to open. I've had trouble adjusting. For one thing, I miss the warm, personal service. Actually, I miss any service. But the idea of self service, with a dearth of clerks and fancy fixtures, is the whole modus of warehouse discount retailing.

Oh, there are a few employees. My observation is about three to the acre. But they are well-trained in warehouse employee school to promote the self-service idea. Answers to queries are met with: "I'm helping another customer, this is not my department, someone will help you in a moment, it's on order, the truck comes Friday, I'm taking inventory, I'm on my break now."

In a decision I'm sure they'll regret, some warehouse managements have provided floor employees with cellular telephones. The idea is sound: Save steps for customers by calling a department a quarter-mile away to find out, say, if 12-2 conduit is available.

But clerks caught on quickly. Now, as soon as you make eye contact with one, his cell phone goes immediately to his ear, followed by rapid, simulated lip movements.

I have found several effective methods for attracting assistance. Pretending you're going to climb on a forklift generally merits notice, as does attempting to remove a product from the bottom of a precarious display of, say, glassware, canned goods, lawn sprinklers, weed killer, or masking tape.

Should you have a question--like where can I find C-clamps-- go in the door marked "staff only." You should find at least two employees in there, drinking coffee and eating Twinkies. Perhaps they'll help you first after their break. If all else fails, go immediately to the outside receiving dock where the help goes to smoke.

Jamming Carts Together

Of course, some employees take smoking breaks outside in front. There they engage in such playful pursuits as jamming shopping carts together, in a manner preventing them from ever being separated. I suspect they also do something with the wheels to cause one of them to lock sideways after you are well into the warehouse.

Discount store personnel have come a long way during the past decade. They were formerly called clerks and paid minimum wage. Now they have titles like associate, partner, or colleague, and they're paid minimum wage. You are now an associate, but try asking for Friday afternoon off.

Incidentally, mall store managements deserve credit for what they are doing for today's youth. Go into any mall boutique, especially in the evening, and you won't see any salesperson over age sixteen and a half.

Millions of dollars in merchandise, thousands more in displays and equipment--all entrusted to one or two eleventh graders. Where are the owners/investors? I don't know. Perhaps in Florida, where they keep track of cash flow and inventory by E-mail or satellite

We're Big

Checkouts in the sooper-dooper stores are sooper-dooper annoyances. Practically all of them have 12 to 15 check stands, equipped with the latest laser-scanning cash registers. This, of course, is to project the idea of bigness. Hey, look at us! Fifteen check stands!

The problem is that only three are open at any one time, and the associate or colleague behind one of these is changing register tape and temporarily closed. Lines behind the other two extend to the rear of store, and odds are the cashier at one is waiting for a price check.

Since all big warehouse retailers are pretty much alike in this respect, the decision on how many registers to open is evidently made at the corporate level in some distant city. Perhaps by the directors. Board member: "The manager of the Sioux Falls store would like to open a fourth register." Board chairman: "Now Claude, you know our policy as well as I do. All together now: 'The more store clerks, the less our perks.'"

Incidentally, all retailers are missing lost sales because they fail to indicate which end of their plastic bags open. If shoppers didn't lose five minutes working on the wrong end of one bag, they would have time to open and fill others.

You do save on delivery costs when you shop the giant retailers. It would have cost $50.00 for delivery of the 250 lb. entertainment center (assembly required) I purchased at U-do-it Depot. Instead, after several failed efforts, I was able to hoist the giant carton to the top of my Toyota Tercel. The resulting chiropractic visit was only $40. That's a solid $10 saving.

If I had to name my favorite place to shop, I guess it would be the giant hardware warehouse stores. Incidentally, these establishments are a boon to the matronly wives of old codger husbands. When such couples were young, the wife could say to her beloved, "If you don't mow the lawn, you'll get no sex tonight." Ah, but that was yesterday. Now, she says, "If you don't mow the lawn, you can't go to Home Depot."

Six Dozen Tube Socks

I also have a passion for the behemoth food and sundries retailers. All offerings come in colossal containers. As a child of the Great Depression, I suffer from a perception of impending doom and deprivation, which a fairly comfortable later life has failed to dispel. Childhood fears die hard.

Those gallon jars of mustard, ketchup, mayonnaise, olives, kidney beans, sliced peaches, and strawberry preserves, safely ensconced in my pantry, after a typical visit to Costco surpass my investment portfolio when it comes to dealing with my insecurity. Ditto the six dozen shrink-wrapped tube socks, and the package of eight dozen "D" batteries I bought last week.

To me, figures on bank and mutual fund statements, as well as those on stock and bond certificates, are just that--cold printing on pieces of paper. But when I glance at my purchases, I say to myself, "Hey guy, you're a success. You've made it. You'll never go without."

Prior to retiring from the business world, George L. Beiswinger enjoyed a long and successful career in corporate communications and public relations. In addition, as a freelancer during that period, he wrote and published more than one hundred articles in various national business magazines, serving as contributing editor to two of those publications. Since retiring, Beiswinger has experimented with various types of humor and satire, which have been published in *The Rotarian, The Lion, Training Magazine, Grit, Catholic Digest,* and several others. A graduate of Washington University, Saint Louis, he received a master's degree in journalism from Temple University, Philadelphia. Beiswinger and his wife, Ginny, live in Mt. Laurel, NJ.